太和武当
武当博物馆·道教文化展
Taihe Wudang
Taoist Culture Exhibition of Wudang Museum

文物出版社

责任印制：王少华
责任编辑：赵　磊
封面设计：黑马文化传播有限公司

图书在版编目（CIP）数据

太和武当 / 李发平主编．--北京：文物出版社，2011.11
　ISBN 978-7-5010-3240-2

　Ⅰ.①太... Ⅱ.①李... Ⅲ.①武当山-道教-宗教文化-图录　Ⅳ.①B958

中国版本图书馆CIP数据核字（2011）第163768号

太和武当

李发平　主编

文物出版社出版发行

（北京东直门内北小街2号楼　邮政编码 100007）
http://www.wenwu.com
E-mail: web@wenwu.com

印制　北京图文天地制版印刷有限公司
经销　新华书店经销
开本　889×1194毫米　1/16
印张　14
版次　2011年11月第1版
印次　2011年11月第1次印刷
书号　ISBN 978-7-5010-3240-2
定价　300.00元

太和武当
武当博物馆·道教文化展
Taihe Wudang
Taoist Culture Exhibition of Wudang Museum

主　　编	李发平
副 主 编	陈平海
执行主编	舒　涛
执行副主编	韩继斌
书稿策划	舒　涛　李光辉　韩继斌　赵本新　徐增林
编委成员	张　剑　熊红伟　唐云龙　刘　琦　郑红梅
	刘　伟　杜　鑫　张　丽　刘　实　陈　锐
	陈　晋　柳　芳　张天清　邓元保　蒋兴锋
	屈　伟　霍　飞　刘　耿　刘　飞　魏　睿
	舒成海　胡江源　沈　斌　陈　聪　熊　波
	石远丽　赵　静　薛　霄　姚俊芳　张婧钰
	饶　蕾　吕　峰　李洋樊
撰　　稿	韩继斌　熊红伟
摄　　影	徐增林　赵本新　韩继斌
翻　　译	张　玫　陈　锐
展览制作	宋沛然　栾东达
封面设计	黑马文化传播有限公司

Chief Editor: Li Faping
Vice Chief Editor: Chen Pinghai
Editorial Member: Shu Tao
Associate Chief Editor: Han Jibin
Planning: Shu Tao Li Guanghui Han Jibin Zhao Benxin Xu Zenglin
Editorial Member: Zhang Jian Xiong Hongwei Tang Yunlong
Liu Qi Zheng Hongmei Liu Wei Du Xin Zhang Li Liu Shi
Chen Rui Chen Jin Liu Fang Zhang Tianqing Deng Yuanbao
Jiang Xingfeng Qu Wei Huo Fei Liu Geng Liu Fei Wei Rui
Shu Chenghai Hu Jiangyuan Shen Bin Chen Cong Xiong Bo
Shi Yuanli Zhao Jing Xue Xiao Yao Junfang Zhang Jingyu
Rao Lei Lv Feng Li Yangfan
Text: Han Jibin Xiong Hongwei
Photographer: Xu Zenglin Zhao Benxin Han Jibin
Translator: Zhang Mei Chen Rui
Exhibition Maker: Song Peiran Luan Dongda
Cover Designer: Heima Cultural Broadcast Co.,ltd

The Wudang Taoist Cultural Exhibition of Wudang Museum owned the reward of best exhibition during 2007 to 2008. This reward is given by the Bureau of National Cultural Relic, Chinese Museum Association and China Cultural Relic Press. It is evaluated every two years in the nationwide.

序

  大岳武当，伟岸而深沉，他以一种无可超越的尊严，仰止太和，俯瞰苍生。岁月的沧桑与天地的造化，曾经的鼎盛尊荣与神秘的厚重积淀，共同蛰伏于此，等待一个玄妙的轮回，重塑一个辉煌的盛典，造就一个伟大的传奇！

  作为中国远古哲学精神与东方智慧价值的巅峰象征，武当山以神秘空灵的武当仙境、玄妙飘灵的武当武术和堪称华夏魂灵的武当文化，谱写了天地乾坤中最壮丽奇美的经典史诗，演绎着山水太极间人文教化传承的和谐之本。联合国教科文组织将武当山古建筑群列入《世界文化遗产名录》时评价说："武当山是世界上最美的地方之一"，"中国的伟大历史，依然留存在武当山。"

  武当山历史悠久，人杰地灵，在岁月的长河中，东西南北文化繁衍、交融，宫廷与民间文化巧妙结合，孕育了丰厚、独特的武当文化体系。他给世人留下了大量的珍贵文物，数量之多，等级之高，质地之全，全国罕见，其中仅国宝级文物就近1000件（套），且大多为宫廷御赐。

  聚7000余国宝家珍，展武当文化之魂。为了更好地弘扬武当文化，保护好武当山遗存的珍贵文化遗产，在国家、省、市等各级领导的高度重视、关心、支持下，特区自筹资金3000余万元，从2005年3月开始动工兴建，历经三年的艰辛，以高标准建成了一座极具武当特色的现代化博物馆，并于2008年4月23日正式向海内外游客免费开放。

  作为公认的道教第一名山，武当山上千年的历史积淀，集中体现了中国的基本哲学精神。作为中华武术和养生学说的标志性圣地，武当文化也反映了中国人对健康、快乐、平安、和谐的现实追求，以及对人与自然和谐共存的思考。

  中华精气神，荟萃武当山。凭借深厚的文化积淀、独特的道家主题、丰富的文物馆藏、精妙的建筑设计、人本的空间布局、先进的技术水平，武当博物馆正致力于成为推广武当文化的公益窗口、弘扬中华和谐精神的全球文化名片。

  领略太极武当，感悟和谐之道，弘扬中华文化。愿《太和武当》（武当博物馆·道教文化展）一书像中华文明使者一样，将武当文化播撒到地球的每一个角落！

李发平
2010年9月

Preface

The Da Yue Wudang, magnificent and beautiful, upholds the idea of Taihe— harmonious in the world. Although going through such a long time, the past flourish and the mysterious sediment still get together waiting an excellent period with glorious grand ceremony and great marvel.

As the peaked symbolize of Chinese original philosophy spirit and the east wisdom value, Wudang Mountain has composed the most glorious epic with its beautiful natural scenery, esoteric elegant Wudang Wushu and the profound Wudang culture. It has also demonstrated the harmonious between the nature and human. When the Ancient Building Complex in Wudang Mountains was inscribed on the World Cultural Heritage List, the UNESCO evaluate it that Wudang Mountain is one of the most beautiful place in the world and the great past of China is still solid in Mountain Wudang.

During the long history, thanks to the convergence of all cultures, especially palace culture combining folk culture comes into the unique Wudang Culture. There are countless unique curiosa with great quantity, high grade and various textures which are rare in the whole nation. Only the national level cultural relics have more than one thousand which mainly bestowed by the palace.

Owning more than seven thousand national treasure which are exhibit the soul of Wudang Culture, to carry forward the Wudang Culture and protect the precious cultural relics, under the great importance and concern attached by the national, provincial and municipal leader at all levels, our Wudang Special Zone raised funds of more than 30 million RMB to build this high standard Wudang Museum which began to be built in March, 2005. Under three-year hard work, Wudang Museum officially opened free of charge to visitors at home and abroad on 23, April 2008.

As the first Taoist mountain accepted by Chinese primeval philosophic Taoist idea, Wudang Mountain with the thousands of years historical sedimentary deposits embody the basic philosophy spirit. As the symbol holy land of Chinese Wushu and the regimen theory, Wudang culture reflects the Chinese pursue the reality idea of health, happiness, safeness and harmony, and also contains the deliberation of the harmonious coexisting between human and nature. The Chinese basic sprit and idea gather in Wudang Mountain. With profound culture, unique Taoist theme, abundant cultural relics, exquisite architectural design, reasonable layout and advanced technique, Wudang Museum is devote to be the window to popularize Wudang cultural value and spread the harmonious idea all over the world.

Sensing Tai Chi Wudang, inspiriting the harmonious and expanding Chinese culture, wish the book *Taihe Wudang — Taoist Culture Exhibition of Wudang Museum* like Chinese civilized messenger to spread Wudang culture all over the world!

Li Faping
September, 2010

前 言

武当山，又名太和山，是我国著名的道教圣地、内家拳发源地、国家首批重点风景名胜区。1994年，武当山古建筑群被列入《世界文化遗产名录》，2006年，武当武术、武当宫观道乐和武当山道教医药、武当山庙会分别被列入国家和省级《非物质文化遗产名录》。

武当山以其绚丽多姿的自然风景、规模宏大的古建筑群、源远流长的道教文化、博大精深的武当武术著称于世。明代武当山被皇室封为"大岳"、"治世玄岳"，以"四大名山皆拱揖，五方仙岳共朝宗"的"五岳之冠"的显赫地位标名于世，被誉为"亘古无双胜境，天下第一仙山"。明成祖朱棣大建武当山，役使军民工匠30万人，历时12年，共建成9宫、8观、36庵堂、72岩庙、39桥、12亭等庞大建筑群。嘉靖年间又增修扩建，绵延140里，形成了世界上最大的宗教建筑群。联合国专家苏明塔加在考察武当山后称赞："中国伟大的历史，依然存留在武当山。"

武当山现存古建筑53处，建筑面积2.7万平方米，建筑遗址9处，占地面积20多万平方米，全部为国家重点文物保护单位，被誉为"中国古代建筑成就的博物馆"。全山保存各类文物近万件（套），数量之多、等级之高、质地之全，国内罕见。武当博物馆从建筑艺术、道教简史、宫观道乐、道教造像、武当武术、医药养生、仙山名人、香俗文化等方面解读武当文化，有些皇室珍品、御赐实物尚属首次展示，力求让观众更好地走进武当，品味武当，领略武当文化的独特魅力。

Foreword

Wudang Mountain, also named Taihe Mountain, is the national famous Taoist Holy Land, the cradle of internal boxing and one of the first key scenic spots of national-level. In 1994, the Ancient Building Complex in Wudang Mountains was inscribed by UNESCO on the World Cultural Heritage List and in 2006, Wudang Wushu, Wudang Taoist music, Taoist medication and traditional Taoist festivals were included into the Non-material Cultural Heritage List of national and provincial level respectively.

Wudang Mountain is renowned for its beautiful natural scenery, magnificent large-scale ancient building complexes, profound traditional Taoist culture and esoteric elegant Wudang Wushu. In Ming Dynasty, the royal family granted it the title "Da Yue" and "Zhi Shi Da Yue" which indicates that it occupied a more prominent position than the four national famed mountains. Well-known as the king mountain among the five outstanding mountains in China, it is praised as "the unexampled fairy land of the world, the first immortal mountain under the heaven." Emperor Zhu Di (1403-1424) of Ming Dynasty paid great attention to Wudang Mountain and built Wudang on a large scale. Under the work of 300 thousand soldiers, workmen and craftsmen, through 12 years, Wudang Mountain shaped 9 palaces, 8 temples, 36 ancestral temples, 72 rock temples, 39 bridges, 12 pavilions etc. During the reign of Emperor Jiajing (1522-1566), repaired and newly-built architecture in Wudang Mountain which extend for about 140 Li became the largest religious building complexes. Sumimtardia, an expert of UNESCO, praised Wudang Mountain after inspecting: "The great past of China is still solid in Mountain Wudang."

Nowadays, Wudang Mountain has preserved 53 ancient buildings with gross floors area of 27 thousand square miles and 9 sites of architecture occupied more than 200 thousand square miles which are all conferred as national units of cultural relic reservation and honored as a museum of Chinese ancient architecture achievements. There are nearly 10 thousand pieces of culture relics which are unique in the country for great quantity, high grade and various textures. Wudang Museum will exhibit Wudang culture from the aspects of architecture, brief history of Taoism, Taoist music, Taoist josses, Wudang Wushu, medical and regime, celebrity with Wudang, pilgrimage culture. Some royal curiosa and objects bestowed by emperors will have their first appearance in the museum. Wudang Museum strived to let visitors learn about Wudang, indulge in Wudang and appreciate its particular culture.

目 录

序/李发平

前 言

第一篇　经典建筑　演绎武当气度 …………………………………… 004

第二篇　创新设计　传承武当文脉 …………………………………… 006

第三篇　精工装修　再铸武当经典 …………………………………… 008

第四篇　丰富展陈　诠释武当传奇 …………………………………… 010

　　　　苍穹星宿　天地玄妙（序厅） ………………………………… 012

　　　　云中故宫　道法自然（建筑艺术厅） ………………………… 018

　　　　仙山名士　灵通天下（仙山名人厅） ………………………… 056

　　　　治世玄岳　鼎盛尊荣（道教造像厅） ………………………… 076

　　　　道教源流　和谐本真（道教简史厅） ………………………… 134

　　　　香俗朝宗　福寿康宁（香俗文化厅） ………………………… 160

　　　　太极祖庭　文明瑰宝（武术养生厅） ………………………… 172

　　　　武当道乐　天籁仙音（宫观道乐厅） ………………………… 192

后 记

Contents

Preface / Li Faping

Foreword

  Ⅰ. Classical Architecture Exhibit Wudang Style ·················· 004

  Ⅱ. Innovative Design Inherit Wudang Culture ·················· 006

  Ⅲ. Fine Decoration Embody Wudang Classic ·················· 008

  Ⅳ. Rich Exhibition Explain Wudang Stories ·················· 010

    Constellation of the Heaven Mysterious World（The Lobby） ············ 012

    The Forbidden City in the Mist Following the Course of Nature

    （Art of Architecture Hall） ·················· 018

    Fairy Mountain and Celebrity Famed to the World

    （Mountain with Celebrities Hall） ·················· 056

    Zhi Shi Xuan Yue Prosperity Period（Taoist Josses Hall） ·················· 076

    The Original Taoism The Harmonious Idea（Taoist History Hall） ······ 134

    Pilgrimage Brings You Wealth, Healthy, Happiness and Longevity

    （Pilgrimage Culture Hall） ·················· 160

    Tai Chi, Cultural Treasure（Wushu and Regimen Hall） ·················· 172

    Wudang Taoist Music Celestial Melody（Taoist Music Hall） ············ 192

Postscript

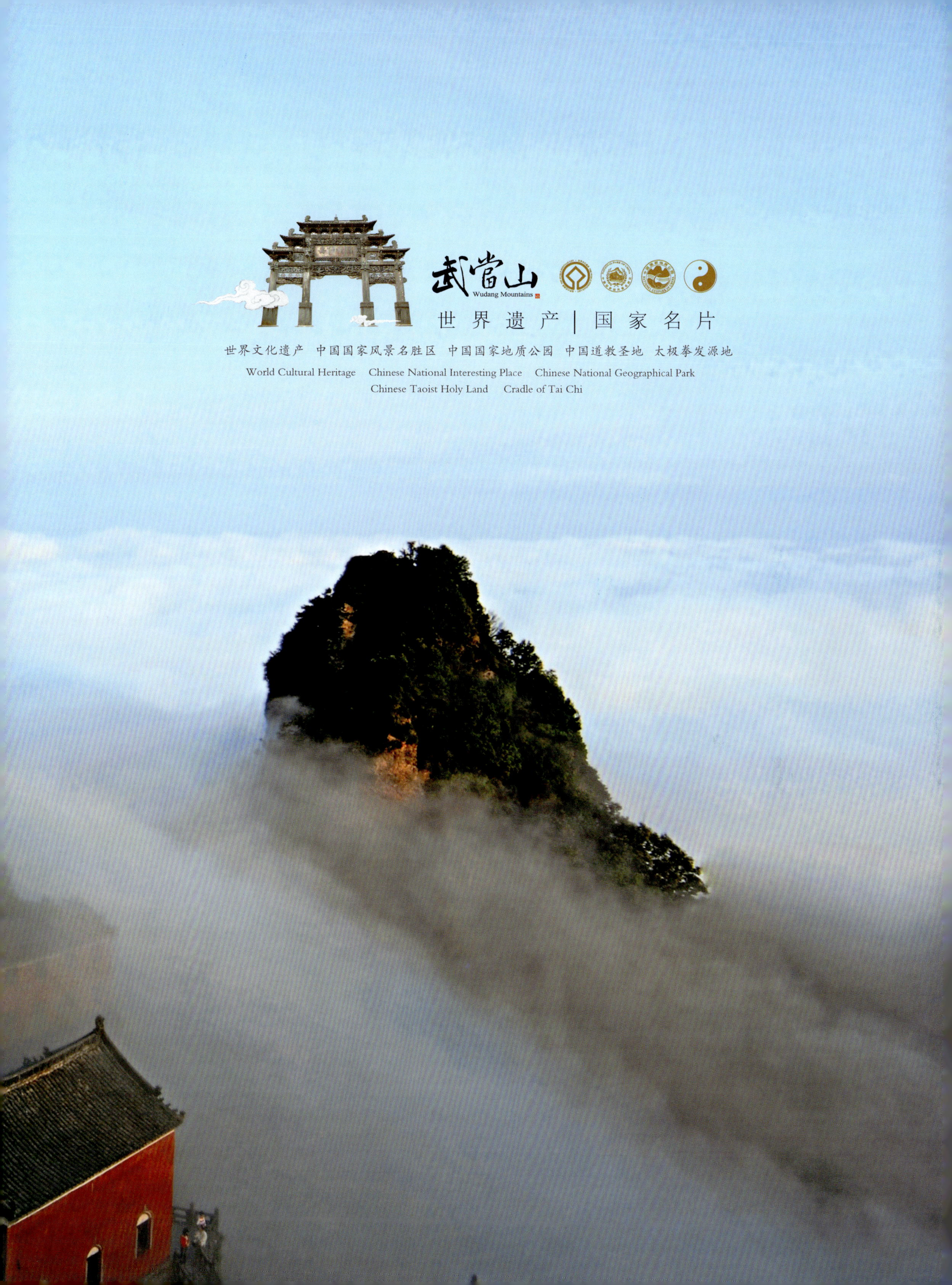

世界文化遗产　中国国家风景名胜区　中国国家地质公园　中国道教圣地　太极拳发源地
World Cultural Heritage　Chinese National Interesting Place　Chinese National Geographical Park
Chinese Taoist Holy Land　Cradle of Tai Chi

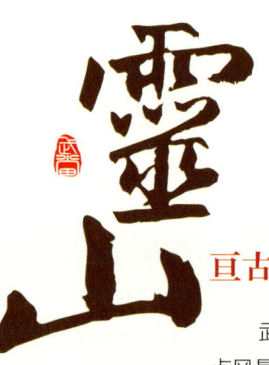

亘古无双胜境 · 天下第一仙山

　　武当山，又名太和山，位于湖北省十堰市境内，是联合国世界文化遗产、国家首批重点风景名胜区和著名的道教文化圣地。

　　神秘空灵的武当仙境、玄妙飘灵的武当武术和堪称华夏魂灵的武当文化，谱写了天地乾坤中最壮丽奇美的经典史诗，演绎着山水太极间人文教化传承的和谐之本，素有"亘古无双胜境，天下第一仙山"的美誉。联合国教科文组织认定武当山列入世界文化遗产名录时评价说："武当山是世界上最美的地方之一"，"中国的伟大历史，依然留存在武当山。"

　　武当博物馆"道教文化展"，凝聚八百里巍巍大岳武当人文精华，穿越浩荡几千年中国道家文化时空。

　　Wudang Mountain which is also named Taihe Mountain, located in Shiyan Municipal City, Hubei province, is the World Culture Heritage by UNSCO, the Chinese national key scenic spots and the famous Taoist Holy Land.

　　Wudang Mountain owns beautiful natural scenery, mysterious Wudang Wushu and the glorious Wudang Culture which just composes a magnificent poem and passes the harmony between human and nature. Wudang Mountain has been praised as "the unexampled fairy land of the world, the first immortal mountain under the heaven." When the experts of UNESCO list Mountain Wudang as the World Culture Heritage, they evaluated Wudang Mountain "The one of the most beautiful place in the world", "The great past of China is still solid in Mountain Wudang."

　　The Taoist culture exhibition of Wudang Museum will display the essence of this holy mountain and its thousands of years of Taoism.

第一篇 经典

经典建筑 演绎武当气度

Classical Architecture Exhibit Wudang Style

经典建筑 演绎武当气度
Classical Architecture Exhibit Wudang Style

  武当博物馆坐落于武当山下中心城区，总投资3000余万元，2005年3月动工兴建，2008年4月23日正式向海内外游客免费开放。整体建筑为地面三层，建筑面积6200平方米，其中展厅面积4419平方米。

  博物馆外观设计采用了橄榄形平面，在两侧具有武当山御碑亭体量造型的角楼烘托下，弧形主入口立面上，宽台阶、高柱廊与厚门楣，建筑表情堂皇大气，建筑语言简洁流畅，前临开阔明堂为太极八卦图案的文化广场，共同组成了具有神圣殿堂感的建筑文化氛围。馆名为中国著名书法家欧阳中石亲笔题写。馆内空间独具匠心地吸收了武当山古建筑群高大崇台的特点和"大壮适形"的风格，在曲成万物中营造了流畅的观展动线和丰富变幻的视觉效果。

  Wudang Museum, located in the urban area of Wudang Special Zone, began to be built in March, 2005 and officially opened free of charge to visitors on 23, April 2008. The total invest is more than 30 million RMB which owns three floors on the ground covered an area of 6200m^2 among which there are 4419m^2 as the exhibition hall.

  The whole Museum design appears like an olive on the plane with two turrets on both sides facing the Cultural Square which are the same as the pavilions for Bixi housing a tablet in Wudnag Mountain. The whole architecture is very stately. The Chinese characters about the name of Wudang Museum handwrite by Ouyang Zhongshi, Chinese famous calligrapher. The space inside have great originality absorbing the characteristic and style of the ancient architecture in Wudang Mountains with lofty platform and fit the atmosphere.

创新设计 传承武当文脉
Innovative Design Inherit Wudang Culture

【第二篇】**创新**

武当博物馆的设计理念，秉承着"天人合一，道法自然"的和谐思想，既突出武当文化特色，也力求文脉清晰，雅俗共赏，充分体现贴近生活、贴近群众、贴近社会的指导思想，以适应不同的观众群体。同时在展陈方式上，突破传统博物馆的说教式、展板式等简单方式，以互动式的参与性理念，充分利用声光电等现代多媒体技术，深入浅出地诠释深奥的道教文化。

武当文化，华夏魂灵。中国近代伟大的文学家鲁迅曾经说过："中国的根柢全在道教。"道教是中国土生土长的宗教，自汉代产生以来，在历史的长河中，经过几千年的交融、积淀、发展，孕育了深厚、丰富的道教文化。武当山作为中国道教的发源地，中国四大道教名山之一，自古以来备受隐居修道之士青睐，加之武当山在中国特殊的地理位置，东西南北文化相互融合、繁衍，一度被朝廷皇权所重视，最终使武当山成为了中国道教"第一山"。

武当博物馆是武当山近年来一项重要的文化工程。在这片古老的土地上，蕴含着说不完的神奇和美妙，延续着中国割不断的文化传承。聚武当7000余件（套）国宝家珍，展武当之灵魂。为使武当山博物馆的展陈设计做到最好，定位更准，经过集思广益，我们针对武当文化的特色，立足于武当文物，创新陈列理念，充分营造了博物馆的个性化氛围。

武当博物馆展厅位于博物馆建筑的二层和三层，展览面积4419平方米，共设八大展厅。游客从武当文化广场登台阶直接进入博物馆的第二层，首先看到的是武当博物馆的序厅，然后按照顺时针方向依次为建筑艺术厅、仙山名人厅；三层依次为道教造像厅、宫观道乐厅、武术养生厅、香俗文化厅、道教简史厅。在展陈设计上，通过留存的文物、文字、图片，结合模型、声光电、多媒体等多种形式向观众展示武当文化的精髓。

    The design idea of Wudang Museum takes the harmonious idea that everything should follow the nature and oneness between heaven and man. Wudang Museum not only want to extrude the characteristic of Wudang culture but also make it clear to suit both refined and popular tastes, following the guiding ideology of closing to the life, the people and the society to fit different people. Meantime, on the way of exhibition, Wudang Museum makes the best of multimedia technology such as sound, light and electricity and the visitors' join in to explain the profound Taoist culture that is diverse from the traditional museums which exhibit in simple terms such as expound mechanically or the exhibition board.

    Wudang culture is the soul of Chinese culture. Luxun, Chinese litterateur of modern times, once said that the Taoism is the root of Chinese culture. The Taoism is the native-born religion of Chinese which come into being in the Han Dynasty. Going through thousands of years, the Taoism has developed profound Taoist culture. Wudang Mountain, as the birth land and one of the Chinese four famous Taoist mountains, is favored by hermits and Taoist priests since ancient times, especially the special location which makes the culture from the four corners of the world integrate and develop. Once upon a time, the royal court has paid great attention to Wudang Mountain, which makes it being the first Taoist mountain in China.

    Wudang Museum is an important cultural project for Wudang Special Zone in recent years. Wudang Mountain has hold more than seven thousand national treasure and other culture relics, containing different miracle and wonder and also inheriting Chinese culture. How to make the Wudang Museum owns the best exhibition and displays the unique feature of Wudang is the first thing we considered. After drawing on the wisdom of the masses, we aimed at the characteristics of Wudang culture and established in Wudang cultural relics with innovative exhibition idea to make it unique.

    Wudang Museum exhibition hall lies on the second and third floor which covered an area of 4419m^2 for eight halls. The visitors first step in the lobby on the second floor, then the architecture hall, mountain with celebrity hall, clockwise; on the third floor, there are Taoist josses hall, Taoist music hall, Wushu and regimen hall, worship culture hall and brief history of Taoism hall. We display the wudang culture through the preserved culture relics, writings, pictures and models.

精工装修 再铸武当经典

Fine Decoration Embody Wudang Classic

博物馆整体装修装饰，大量采用进口米黄砂岩和实木材料，通过"软"、"硬"结合，配以祥和的灯光，既凸现了庄严厚重的皇家气度，也体现了简洁典雅的艺术气质。围绕道教文化主题，微观上又以青龙、白虎、朱雀、玄武四灵和太极文化符号隐于其中，精妙和谐，恰到好处。

The whole decoration of the Museum mostly use the import cream-colored sandstone and solid wood with peaceful lighting that shows the solemn royal style and also embody the elegant artistic features. With the theme of Taoist culture, exquisitely and harmoniously use the four Taoist culture signs—green dragon, white tiger, rosefinch and Xuanwu and also the culture of Tai Chi.

精工装修 再铸武当经典 008-009
Fine Decoration Embody Wudang Classic

太和武当
武当博物馆·道教文化展

建筑艺术厅 Art of Architecture Hall

第四篇

丰富

丰富展陈 诠释武当传奇

Rich Exhibition Explain Wudang Stories

　　武当博物馆分别从建筑艺术、仙山名人、道教造像、道教简史、香俗文化、宫观道乐、武术养生等方面解读武当文化，部分皇室珍品、御赐实物均属独家展示，主线清晰，内容丰富，既是武当山景区游览的补充延续，也是武当文化的深度解读。

　　The Wudang Mueseum will show Wudang culture from the aspect of architecture, mountain with celebrity, Taoist josses, brief history of Taoism, Pilgrimage Culture, Taoist music, Wushu and regimen. Part of the royal treasures and granted relics will have their first appearance to visitors with clear theme and rich content. They are not only the extension of traveling the mountain, but also the fine explanation of Wudang culture.

F2　二层平面布置图　PLAN OF THE SECOND FLOOR

- 仙山名人展厅 CELEBRITY AND WUDANG
- 建筑艺术展厅 ART OF ARCHITECTURE
- 贵宾接待室 DISTINGUISHED GUEST RECEPTION
- 楼梯 STAIRCASE
- 游人休息区 RESTING ROOM
- 卫生间 WASH ROOM
- 纪念品商店 SOUVENIR SHOP
- 存包处 DEPOSITORY
- 咨询台 INFORMATION DESK

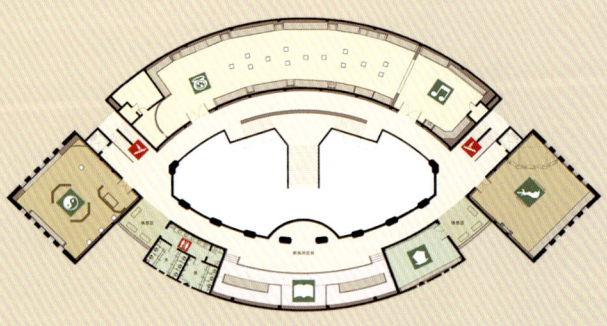

F3　三层平面布置图　PLAN OF THE THIRD FLOOR

- 道教简史展厅 BRIEF HISTORY OF TAOISM
- 道教造像展厅 TAOIST JOSS
- 武术养生展厅 WUSHU WITH REGIME
- 民俗展厅 FOLK CULTURE
- 宫观道乐展厅 TAOIST MUSIC
- 茶室 TEA ROOM
- 电梯 ELEVATOR
- 卫生间 WASH ROOM

仙人名人厅　Mountain with Celebrities Hall

武术养生厅　Wushu and Regimen Hall

香俗文化厅　Pilgrimage Culture Hall

道教造像厅　Taoist Josses Hall

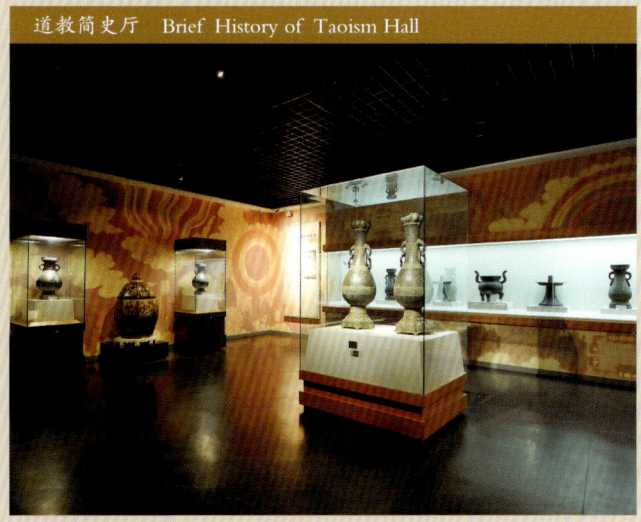
道教简史厅　Brief History of Taoism Hall

宫观道乐厅　Taoist Music Hall

苍穹·星宿 · 天地玄妙
Constellation of the Heaven   Mysterious World

序 厅
The Lobby

武当的"神秘、神奇、神圣"魅力，在您步入武当博物馆挑空大厅的时候，就得到了震撼性的表达。高大穹窿顶，斗、牛、女、虚、危、室、壁七宿居于正中，二十八宿繁星闪烁，威耀寰宇。六甲星神下凡值日，气势磅礴地侍列两侧，目光炯炯，英姿勃发，犹如天兵军阵仪仗，列队迎宾。一座梦想中久别重逢的宫殿，穿越时空在这里与您实现精神邂逅。

When step into the lobby of the Wudang Museum, you will feel the charming of Wudang by its mysterious, miraculous and sacred charming. Looking up, you see 28 lights scattered on the roof which represent the 28 constellations. The middle steps to the third floor, there are six protection Gods standing on both sides as if the celestial army greet you in line.

太和武当
武当博物馆·道教文化展

【北方星宿】

在序厅的顶部,顶灯并不是按照规则的顺序安装的,初看似乎有些杂乱,实际上它是按照中国古代二十八星宿中的北方七宿来分布的,即斗、牛、女、虚、危、室、壁七宿。

二十八宿是我国古代天文学家为了观测天象及日、月、五星的运行,把太阳和月亮所经天区的恒星分成二十八个星座,又将其平均分为四组,每组七宿,分别为东苍龙、西白虎、南朱雀、北玄武(龟蛇合称),亦称为"四象"、"四灵"。道教将二十八宿合成的四象尊崇为护卫神,其中的玄武神自宋以后独受尊崇,地位显赫,被封为玄天上帝,即真武神。由于真武由北方水神到南方修仙的传说故事与明朝永乐皇帝由北京攻打到南京后坐镇天下的故事极为相似,故朱棣在武当大建道场,宣扬"君权神授"、"天人合一"的思想。永乐皇帝实际上是利用它以神化皇权。

青龙
Green Dragon

白虎
White Tiger

朱雀
Rose Finch

玄武
Xuan Wu

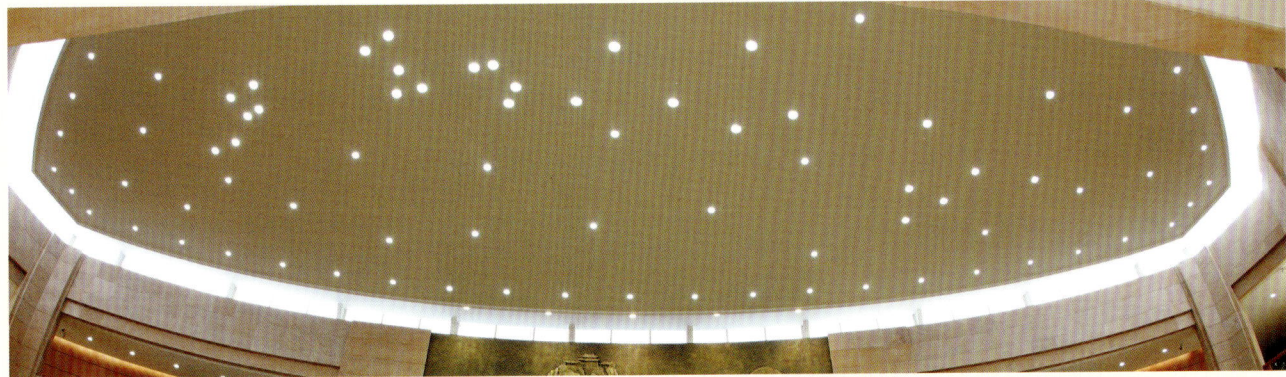

The constellation of the North Sky

On the top of the lobby, for the first eyesight, it seems that the ceiling lamps are installed disorderly. Actually, they are distributed in accordance with the seven north constellations of those 28 in the ancient China, and they are Dou, Niu, Nv, Xu, Wei, Shi and Bi.

The 28 constellations are used as symbols for the purpose of observing the astronomical phenomena and the movement of the sun, the moon, and the five stars by ancient Chinese. And they also averagely divided those 28 constellations into four groups, with seven constellations in one group. They are the Green Dragon in the east, the White Tiger in the west, the Rosefinch in the south, and the Xuanwu (the combination of tortoise and snake) in the north, also being called "Four Xiang" or "Four Ling". Taoism honored the Four Xiang as the guardian gods, in which the Xuanwu god was uniquely worshiped since the Song Dynasty, with a high status, promoted as the Xuantian Heaven Emperor which is also called the Zhenwu God. Since the extreme similarity between the legend that the north water God Zhenwu to the south for cultivating deity and the story of Yongle Emperor's commanding the world in the Ming Dynasty after the attacking of Nanjing from Beijing, the Empore Zhudi constructed the Taoist rites in a large scale in the Wudang Mountains, advocating the thinking of "divine right of kings" and "integration of nature and man" that actually Emperor Yongle has taken advantage of it in order to deify his imperial power.

六甲神

道教祀奉的星神，属紫微垣的六颗星（位于北天星宿中央），分别为甲子神王文卿、甲戌神展子江、甲申神扈文长、甲午神韦玉卿、甲辰神孟非卿、甲寅神明文章。在武当山道教宫观中，六甲神常侍卫在玄天上帝旁边，作为侍卫部将，亦可为保护神。六甲站像雕铸形象来源于生活而高于生活，造型逼真，神态各异，形如真人，为明代皇帝敕谕工部铸造，安奉武当山宫观的国家级珍品。

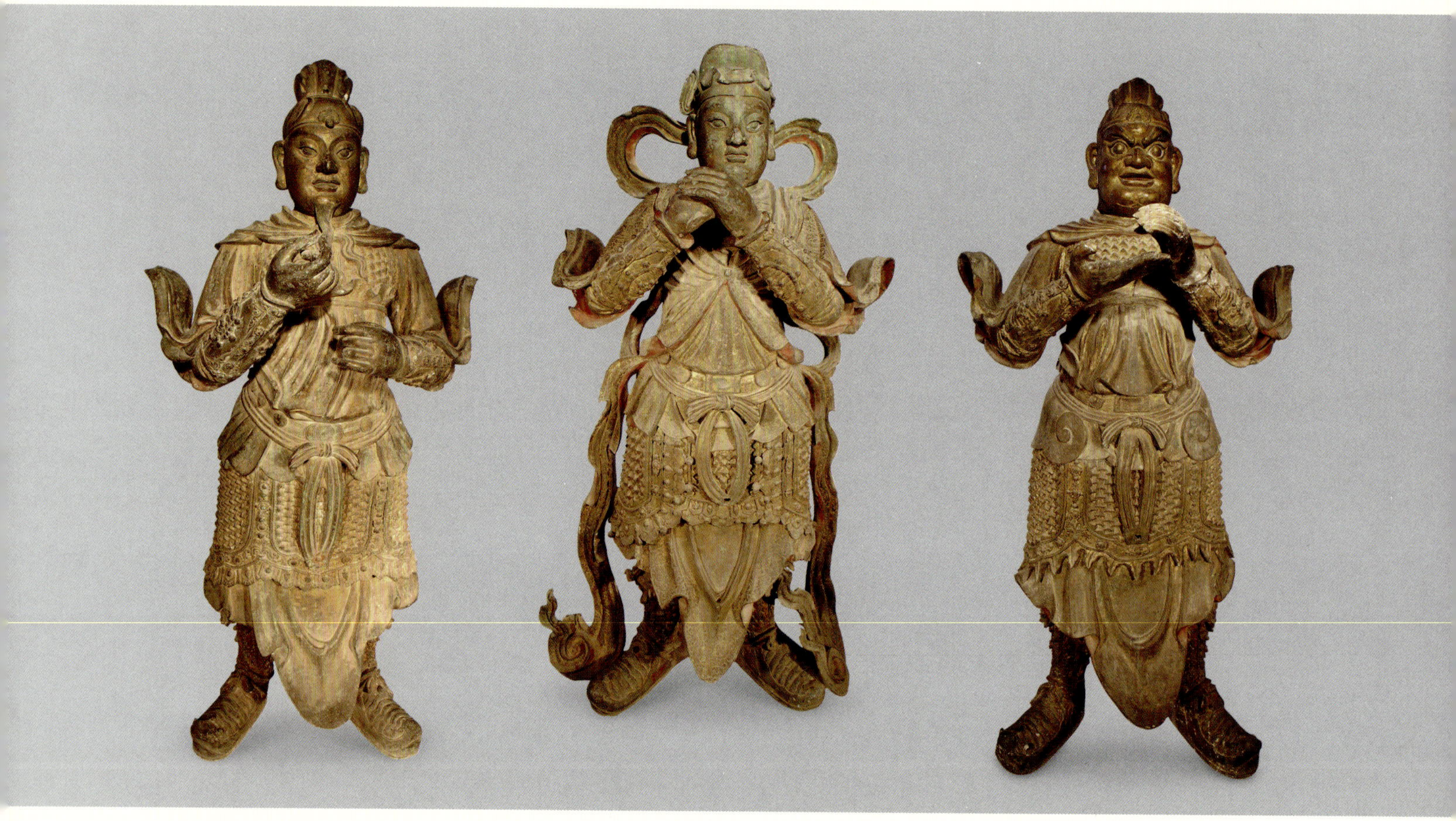

【六甲站像一】

明，铜铸鎏金，像高195.5cm，宽98cm，重2085kg。原存武当山玄都宫。该站像头顶梳髻，无冠，身着铠甲，双臂弯曲伸于胸前，双脚踏战靴呈外八字形站立。

Standing Sculpture of the Six "Jia"

Standing Sculpture of the Six "Jia" is made in Ming Dynasty, copper gilding, 195.5cm height, 98cm wide and weight 2085kg. This sculpture comes from the Xuandou Palace. He has topknot on his head without hat wearing armor. His arms bend stretching before chest wearing caliga standing shaping like Chinese character "eight".

【六甲站像二】

明，铜铸鎏金，像高192.5cm，宽104cm，重2199kg。原存武当山玄都宫。该站像身着铠甲，飘带飞逸，头戴狮子盔，浓眉大眼，嘴巴微张，两手相握抱于胸前，双脚踏战靴呈外八字形站立，似向人致敬状。

Standing Sculpture of the Six "Jia"

Standing Sculpture of the Six "Jia", made in Ming Dynasty, copper gilding, 192.5cm tall, 104cm wide and weight 2199kg. This sculpture comes from the Xuandou Palace. He wears armour and lion-like helmet. He has a square face, thick eyebrow and big eyes with month open. Hands hold before chest wearing caliga just looking like pay a tribute to others.

【六甲站像三】

明，铜铸鎏金，像高195.5cm，宽97.5cm，重2111kg。原存武当山玄都宫。该站像头顶梳髻，身着铠甲，左手残佚，右手拇指残损，双手似捧物状伸于胸前，双脚踏战靴呈外八字形站立。

Standing Sculpture of the Six "Jia"

Standing Sculpture of the Six "Jia", made in Ming Dynasty, copper gilding, 195.5cm tall, 97.5cm wide and weight 2111kg. This sculpture comes from the Xuandou Palace. He splayed his feet wearing caliga, topknot on his head without hat, wearing armour. His hand has been broken just looking like hold something before chest.

Six Jia (Gods)

The God of stars deified by Taoism, belong to the six stars of Ziweiyuan (the center of the constellation in the north sky). They are the Jiazi God, Wang Wenqin, the Jiaxu God, Zhan Zijiang, the Jiashen God, Hu Wenchang, the Jiawu God, Wei Yuqin, the Jiachen God, Meng Feiqin, and the Jiayin God, Ming Wenzhang. In the Taoist palace and temple of the Wudang Mountains, the Six Jia Gods usually guard beside the Xuantian Heaven Emperor Zhenwu, as guarding generals, also called protector gods. The statue of the six Jias originates from life, but they are more artistic, with vivid image, diversified facial expressions, and the real-man shape. It was made to put in palaces and temples of Wudang Mountain by the Ministry of Works belonging to the royal command by the emperors of the Ming Dynasty. It is classified as the national-level precious article in the Wudang Mountains.

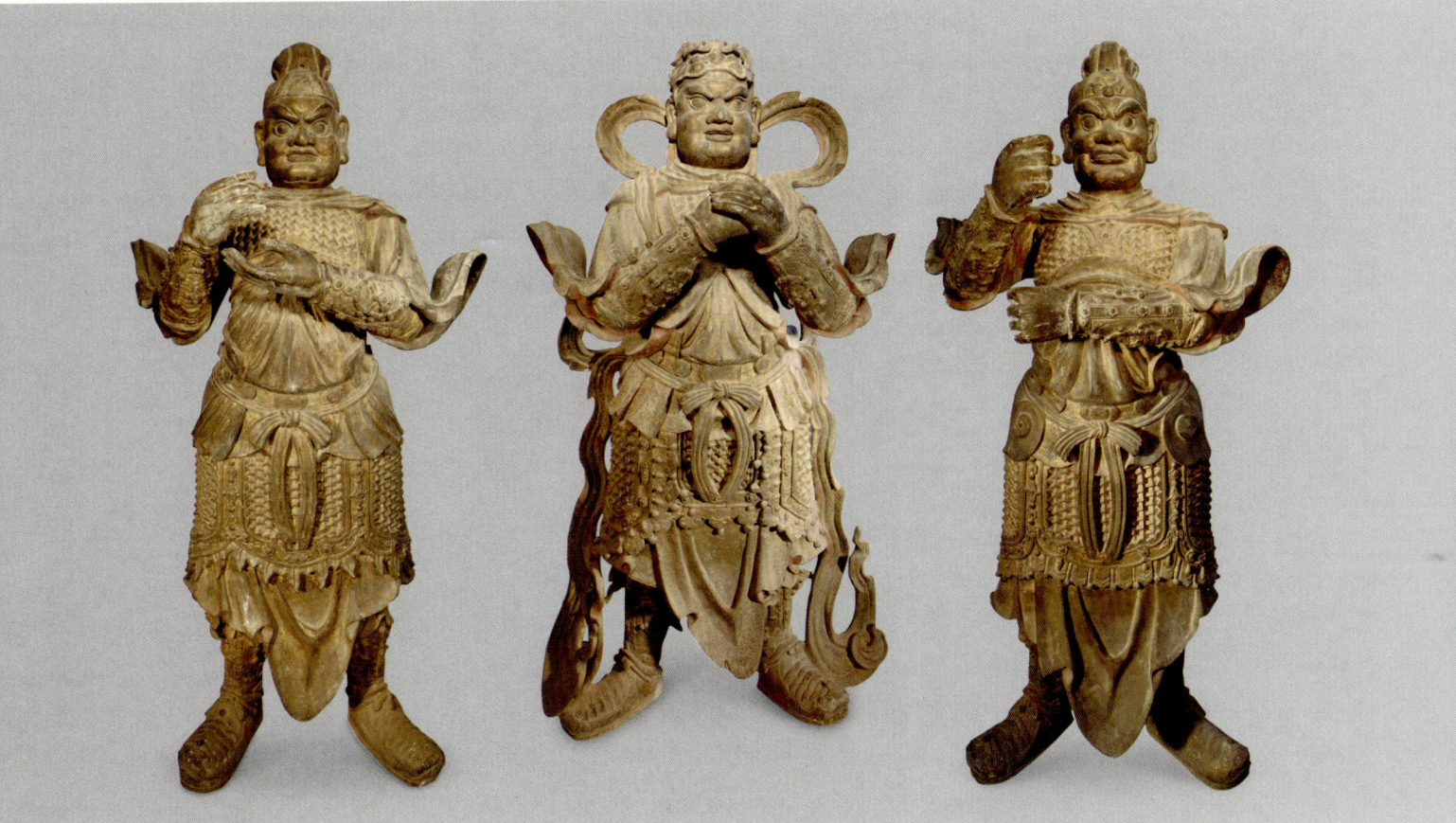

【六甲站像四】
明，铜铸鎏金，像高195cm，宽102cm，重1980kg。该站像头顶梳髻，身着铠甲，双手似捧物状伸于胸前，双脚踏战靴呈外八字形站立。

Standing Sculpture of the Six "Jia"

Standing Sculpture of the Six "Jia", made in Ming Dynasty, copper gilding, 195cm tall, 102cm wide and weight 1980kg. The topknot on his head without hat but wears armour. His hands stretched before his chest just looking like holding small things. He wears caliga standing shaping like Chinese character "eight".

【六甲站像五】
明，铜铸鎏金，像高190cm，宽104.5cm，重2088kg。该站像头戴狮子盔，身着铠甲，飘带飞逸，双手握拳伸于胸前，似致敬状，双脚踏战靴呈外八字形站立。

Standing Sculpture of the Six "Jia"

Standing Sculpture of the Six "Jia", made in Ming Dynasty, copper gilding, 190cm tall, 104.5cm wide and weight 2088kg. He wears lion-like helmet and armour. He just looks like pay a tribute to someone. He wears caliga standing shaping like Chinese character "eight".

【六甲站像六】
明，铜铸鎏金，像高198cm，宽93.5cm，重1992kg。该站像头顶梳髻，身着铠甲，两手似执旗状伸于胸前右侧，双脚踏战靴呈外八字形站立。

Standing Sculpture of the Six "Jia"

Standing Sculpture of the Six "Jia", made in Ming Dynasty, copper gilding, 198cm tall, 93.5cm wide and weight 1992kg. He wears topknot and armour. His hands just like holding the flag. He wears caliga standing shaping like Chinese character "eight".

云中故宫·道法自然

The Forbidden City in the Mist Following the Course of Nature

建筑艺术厅
Art of Architecture Hall

  武当山古建筑群是以唐、宋、元三朝建筑为基础，以明初大规模兴建的皇家庙观为主体的古建筑群。总体规划严密、主次分明、大小有序、布局合理，建筑注重环境选择，讲究山形地脉，聚气藏风，与自然高度和谐，是具有天才创造力的规划与建筑杰作，体现了人文和自然景观完美天成的结合。武当山古建筑形式多样，涵盖了明朝所有的建筑形制，工艺精良，用材考究，在中国乃至世界上都是绝无仅有的实物例证。武当山古建筑群的大兴，是明永乐皇帝用武力夺取政权后大修文治的重要例证，也是《明史》中记述的"靖难之役"、"壬寅宫变"两个重大政治事件的产物。朱棣在对外实施扩展外交政策的同时对内大力推崇武当道教，利用"太子修仙"的神话凝聚民众，向天下宣扬"君权神授"、"天人合一"的思想，以巩固皇权，有着重大的历史意义和社会意义。

  建筑艺术展厅系统诠释了武当山古建筑群的沧桑变迁和非凡的艺术价值，以及对今天的重要启示。

  最引人入胜的就是明代三十万军民大建武当的场景再现，集绘画、人物塑像、建筑造景、音乐动画、声光幻影等多种表现手法于一体，气势恢弘，生动逼真，震撼人心。

  The Ancient Building Complex in Wudang Mountains, based on the architecture of Tang, Song and Yuan Dynasties, mainly consist of the royal temples and palaces built in the early Ming Dynasty. They are all the outstanding architectural masterpieces of genius and creative planning with precise overall layout, clear distinction between the major and minor parts, proper order of larger and smaller parts, and proper shaped layout. The environment of the architecture is out of exquisite selection and harmonious with the nature. The ancient architecture in Wudang Mountain show variety in types, almost covering all the architecture forms of Ming Dynasty with fine craftwork and high techniques and using materials of good quality. They are works of being unique and rare in China and also in the world. The construction of the ancient building complex in Wudang Mountain presented itself as an example of Emperor Yongle of Ming Dynasty, who seized the crown by means of force and started construction in terms of culture and architecture. It was the product of such major political happenings as the "Jingnan Battle"and "Renwu Sacrifice". Emperor Zhu Di advocated Wudang Taoism at home while expanded his foreign policy, cohered people by the myth of the prince cultivated to become the deity and preached the idea of "the emperor's power was granted by god" and "heaven and man combined in one", which consolidated his power with an important social and historical meaning.

  The Architecture Hall interprets the long-term changes and extraordinary artistic value of the Ancient Building Complex in Wudang Mountains and also gives us some important enlightenment of Ancient Building Complex in Wudang Mountains for today.

  The most interesting one is the reappear scene of three hundred thousand persons construct Wudang on a large scale

世界文化遗产——武当山古建筑群
World Cultural Heritage the Ancient Building Complex in the Wudang Mountains

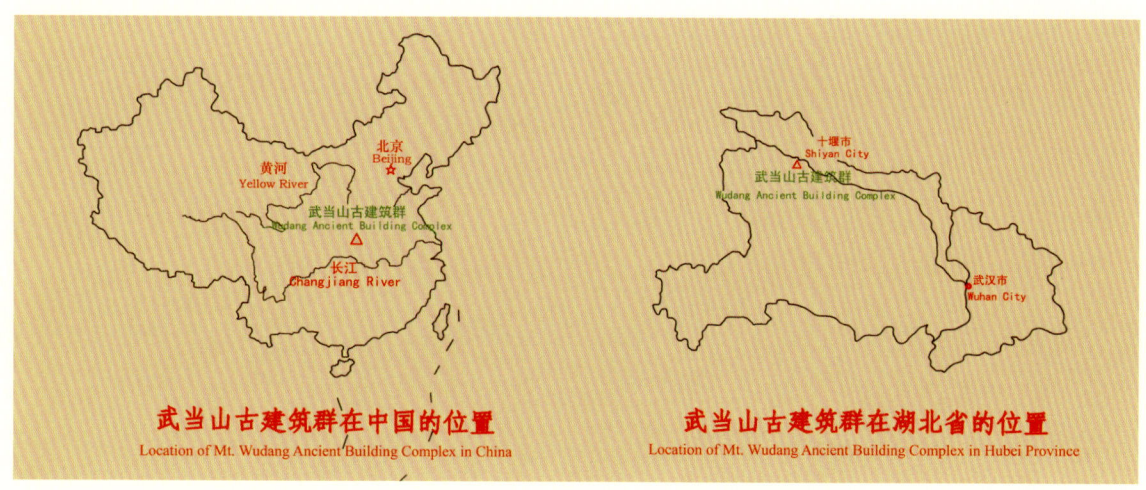

武当山古建筑群在中国的位置
Location of Mt. Wudang Ancient Building Complex in China

武当山古建筑群在湖北省的位置
Location of Mt. Wudang Ancient Building Complex in Hubei Province

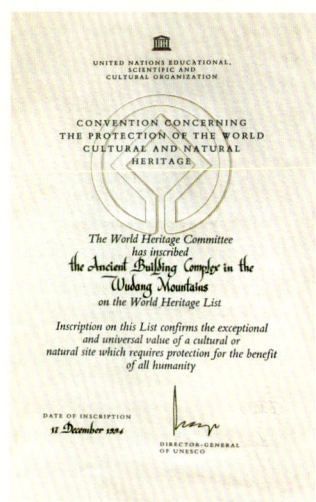

1956年至1996年，武当山部分建筑先后被国务院公布为全国重点文物保护单位、国家级重点风景名胜区。1994年12月15日，武当山古建筑群被联合国教科文卫组织列入《世界文化遗产名录》。2006年，国务院将武当山古建筑群全部公布为全国重点文物保护单位。

From 1956 to 1996, part of the ancient buildings in Wudang Mountain were conferred successively as national units of cultural relic reservation and the key scenic spots of national-level by State Council of the P.R.C. on 15th December, 1994, the Ancient Building Complex in Wudang Mountains was inscribed by UNESCO on the World Cultural Heritage List. In 2006, all of the ancient buildings in Wudang Mountain were conferred as national units of cultural relic reservation by State Council of the P.R.C.

武当山古建筑群是中国古代建筑的优秀文化遗产，尤其是明朝永乐皇帝御赐的金殿，更是凝聚了中国古代建筑技术的精华，代表我国十五世纪科学技术和铸造工艺的重大发展。1994年联合国教科文专家考斯拉考察武当山时说到："武当山自然是世界上最美的地方之一。因为这里融汇了古代的智慧、历史的建筑和自然的美景。对我个人来说，这三个非常重要的方面，为居住在都市和现代氛围中的人，提供了一个天然、宁静的场所。"

The Ancient Building Complex in the Wudang Mountains is the precious cultural heritage in Chinese ancient architecture, especially the Golden Palace which was decreed to be built by the Empeor Yongle of Ming Dynasty, converged the quintessence of Chinese ancient architecture techniques, representing the great development of science technic and casting industry of the 15th century. Kaosla, an expert of UNESCO, once said when he inspected Wudang Mountain that: "Mt. Wudang area is certainly one of the most beautiful areas in the world because it combines ancient wisdom, historic architecture and natural beauty. There are to me the three most important aspects of providing peace and tranquility, for people living in urban and modern environment."

历史悠久 ◎ 人间仙境
Long History　World Fairyland

历史沿革
Historical Evolution

　　作为中国道教的早期活动场所，中国四大道教名山之一，武当山自古以来就受到了隐居修道之士的青睐，加之武当山在中国特殊的地理位置，东西南北文化相互融合、繁衍，自唐以来又一直被朝廷所重视，最终使武当山成为了中国道教第一名山。

　　As one of the four famous Taoist mountains in China, the earlier Taoist activities place, Wudang Mountain was favored by hermits and people who wants to cultivate oneself. Thanks to its particular geographical location, the culture from all sides met and developed in Wudang Mountain especially since the Tang Dynasty, the royal family attached great importance to Wudang Mountain which made it become the first famous Taoist mountain in China.

太和宫　Taihe Palace

朝代	年代	文献记录	现存史料
新石器时代	6700年前	已有人类活动	考古发现
周	公元前770~476年	尹喜在武当筑石室修炼	《舆地纪胜》
楚	公元前616年	周顷王3年，楚灭麇国后武当归楚	《图经》
秦	公元前272年	秦昭王35年置南阳郡，其地属焉	《史记》
汉	公元前202年	汉高祖5年置武当县，属南阳郡	《均州志》
三国	221年	魏文帝黄初2年仍置武当县，属南乡郡	《均州志》
晋	280~289年	晋武帝太康年间，武当县属荆州顺阳郡	《均州志》
南北朝	420~589年	武当归属变动频繁	《均州志》
隋	585年	隋文帝开皇5年改平州为均州，领武当县	《均州志》
唐	贞观初年	敕建五龙祠	《太和山志》等
宋	真宗时期	升五龙祠为五龙观，敕建南岩宫	《太和山志》等
元	1260~1327年	大修武当宫观	志书、建筑、碑刻
明	1412年、1552年	大规模营建、扩建武当山	志书、实物

皇家宫观 ◎ 飞龙天降
Royal Temples and Palaces　Dragon-shaped Layout

规划特色
Planning Characteristics

　　武当山古建筑群分布在以天柱峰为中心的群山之中，总体规划严密、主次分明、大小有序、布局合理。建筑位置注重环境选择，讲究山形水脉、聚气藏风，并考虑了各建筑单元的间距疏密。具体建筑设计规制严谨，或宏伟壮观、或小巧精致、或深藏山坳、或濒临险崖，都十分注重与环境的相互补益，具有浓郁的建筑韵律，达到了建筑与自然的高度和谐，是具有天才创造力的规划与建筑杰作。

　　The Ancient Building Complex in the Wudang Mountains distribute among the hills centralized by Tianzhu Peak with strict overall plan, clear difference between the major and minor parts and a proper order between the large and small parts. The architecture shows a careful selection on the environment and the shape of mountains and terrain. It pays great attention to the collection of Qi and wind, a harmonious relationship with nature and takes the distance between different building units into consideration. The detail design and overall plan are very scrupulous, some are grand and magnificent, some are exquisite and lovely, some are hiding in the woods, and some are standing on the cliffs. No matter how they are look like, they all accord with the environment and possess a constructional style. The buildings, made in harmony with their surroundings that the line between architecture and nature seems nowhere apparent, are the outstanding architecture masterpieces of genius and creative planning.

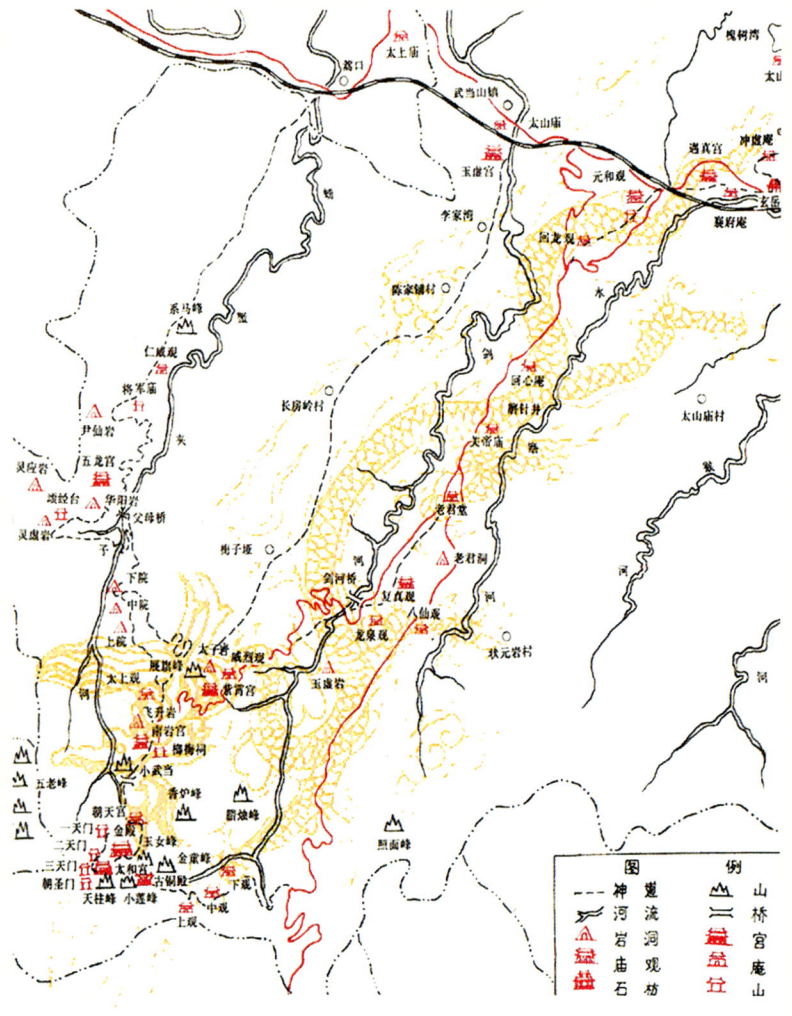

南修武当 ◎ 北建故宫
Construct Wudang Architecture in South　Build Summer Palace in North

建筑辉煌
Splendid Architecture

永乐帝大修武当
Emperor Yongle Built Wudang on a Large Scale

明永乐十年（1412）二月，朱棣颁旨命道录司右正一孙碧云前往武当山实地勘测，同年六月，规划工作就绪。七月十一日，永乐皇帝再颁《敕官员军民夫匠人等》圣旨，为大力修建武当宫观发出了最高动员令，并正式开工建设。

In February the 10th year of Ming Yongle Reign (1412A.D.), the Emperor Zhu Di decreeded to dispatch the official Sun Biyun to explore in Wudang Mountain.In June of the same year, the layout was finished and on July 11, Emperor Yongle issued Imperial Decree to his officials, civilians and artisans which was the highest mobilizable order for building Taoist palaces and temples and began the construction in Wudang Mountain.

明永乐皇帝像
Portrait of Emperor Yongle

武当山现存圣旨较多，其中仅明永乐皇帝向武当山下旨就达600多道。现存圣旨中石雕圣旨有十座，木雕圣旨有三通，非常珍贵。其中木圣旨均为皇宫所送，其底版均为百年银杏制作，边框为杉木，圆首，朱红底，金字，顶部呈半弧形，中部楷书阴刻永乐皇帝禁令，边框四周设九条行龙，背面边框装饰阴线团云图案。据已故国家文物专家朱家溍教授考证，制作此圣旨牌共需83道工序，制作工艺非常考究，为武当文物珍品，镇库之宝。

There are still many extant imperial edicts in Wudang Mountain, among which there are more than 600 edicts decreed by Emperor Yongle. There are ten stone-made and three wooden imperial edicts in stock which are very precious. Those wooden imperial edicts, which came from imperial palace, have been made of hundred-year gingko with fir-made frame. The wooden edicts have golden Chinese characters in vermilion; on the top, it shaped as semiarch; in the middle, it engraved the Emperor Yongle's Prohibition; around the edge of the frame, nine dragons were carved and in the back, it decorated the pattern of Yin Xian Tuan Yun. According to the research of professor Zhu Jiajin, a national cultural relic expert, there are 83 working procedures in making this kind of imperial edict and its making craft are very elegant. It is priceless cultural relic and rare treasure of Wudang Museum.

永乐皇帝大修武当圣旨
Emperor Yongle's Imperial Decree about building Wudang on a large scale

博大精深 ◎ 古建精华
Profound and Prosperous Culture　　Essence of Ancient Architecture

建筑艺术
Art of Architecture

结合自然环境　造成玄妙境界
Combine the Natural Environment　　Form the World Fairyland

1、永乐皇帝大修武当，为保护武当原始生态，下令严禁砍伐树木。凡建筑所需木材均派专人赴陕西、河南、山西、四川等地购置，供武当山建筑使用。

2、抽调全国著名"阴阳典术"风水师王敏和陈羽鹏等，察勘风水，由皇家设计大师蒯祥主导设计。

3、武当建筑与自然和谐，山水川谷，远取其势，近取其质，宫观庙祠，适形而止，具有天人合一、神奇宁静之美。

Ⅰ. To protect the primitive ecology, when built Wudang, the emperor Yongle forbad deforestation in Wudang Mountain. All woods needed for architecture should be purchased from other places such as Shanxi, Henan, Shanxi and Sichuan.

Ⅱ. Designate famous Yin Yang Scholar Fengshui experts Wang Min, Chen Yupeng etc. to examine the Fengshui (in choosing a site and design for a building, both ideological and practical works are carefully balanced). And appoint the famous designer Kuai Xiang who designed the Summer Palace to design.

Ⅲ. The existing architecture in Wudang Mountain and its natural surroundings are harmonious, the appearance of the remote mountains and rivers have been taken into consideration; for the near ones, the quality has been considered. The temples were built in an appropriate position. They not only show the idea of man and nature are an unity, but also an acquiescent and magical beauty.

天人合一　道法自然
Heaven and Man Combined in One　　The Ways of "Tao" by Nature

1、道教崇信万物回归自然。天、地、人为一个和谐整体，是武当山建筑群的一大特点。

2、武当山地质构造复杂，它运用"自然和谐"的法则来规划，使天、地、人"守道而行"，宫观庙堂"皆得其所"。

Ⅰ.Taoism believe in the truth of everything returns to nature. The heaven, earth and man are the harmonious unit which is one major feature of the Taoist architectures in Wudang Mountain.

Ⅱ.The geologic structure in Wudang Mountain is complicated. It was planned on the principle of "harmonious nature" which means a harmonious trinity of man, earth and heaven. Thus, the heaven, earth and man keep their own natural way and the Taoist temples and palaces have the right place where they belong to.

结构精巧　法式规范
Exquisite Structure　　Standard Construction

武当建筑因地制宜，依山就势，建筑手法独具武当山特有的个性，成为建筑学上的经典。金顶紫金城、南岩宫、太子坡、紫霄宫、玉虚宫等均是极好的例证。

The construction techniques have a unique characteristic of Wudang Mountain built as circumstances permit and following the shape of mountain, which become the classical examples in architecture. The extremely good illustrations are the Forbidden City in the Golden Palace, the South Crag Palace, the Prince Slope, the Purple Heaven Palace, the Yuxu Palace etc.

建筑艺术厅 024-025
Art of Architecture Hall

南岩宫　（摄影:张兴）
South Crag Palace　（Photographer: Zhang Xing）

构思奇妙　巧夺天工
Marvelous Idea　Wonderful Workmanship

武当山古建筑群由皇帝亲自策划营建，特别是在明朝，武当山的建设均由皇室派员管理。其建筑规模之大、规制之高、构造之严谨、装饰之精美、神像供器品类之多，在中国现存的建筑中都是绝无仅有的，在世界上也是独特的、稀有的。

The Ancient Building Complex in Wudang Mountains was planned to build by the emperors, especially in the Ming Dynasty, the royal family sent officials to overlook the construction in Wudang Mountain. Those architectures are the unique illustrations of Chinese extant architectures for their magnificent scale, high-standard planning, rigorous construction, delicate decoration and various Taoist josses and sacrificial vessels which are also unique and rare in the world.

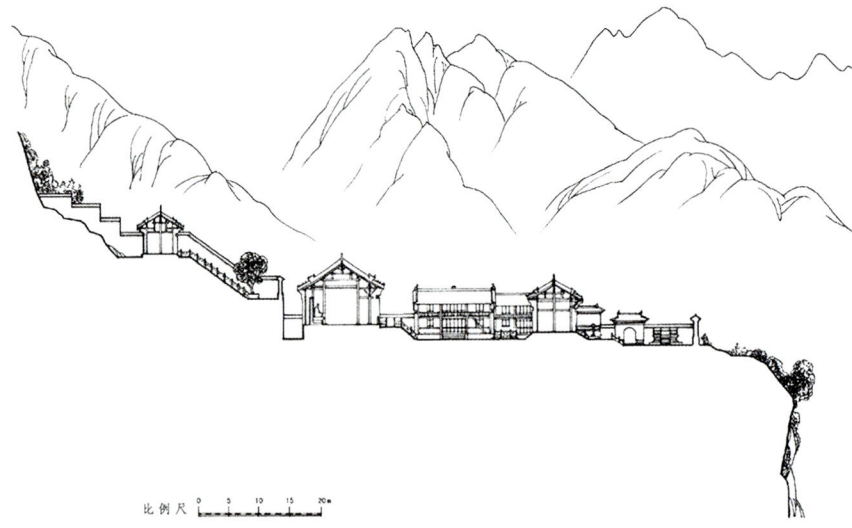

武当山复真观剖面图
Section of Fuzhen Temple

  复真观，又名太子坡，系在陡坡、陡岩、险壁上序列布局建起的一组建筑，是武当山现存最完整的观宇，其依山就势修建的一处曲折复道，被称为九曲黄河墙，其势、其意及回音效果，均可与北京天坛相媲美。

  Fuzhen Temple is also named the Prince Slope. It was an architecture group which built on slope, crag and precipice with well-organized layout. It is the only well preserved temple in Wudang Mountains. The zigzag path, named the Nine-winding Yellow River Walls, was built following the precipice. Its momentum, meaning and echo effects can rival the Temple of Heaven in Beijing.

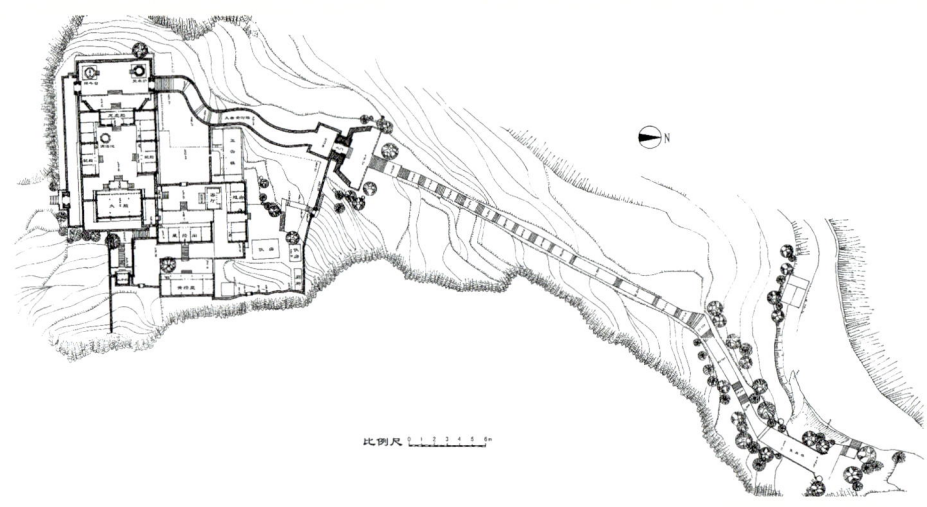

武当山复真观平面图
Plan of Fuzhen Temple

  古代宫殿建筑形式很多，但其复杂的部位均在两侧。对两端不同的处理，形成不同的艺术形式和不同的命名，武当山古建筑群的建筑形式丰富多样，涵盖了所有古代建筑的形式风格，堪称是一座中国古代宫殿建筑的博物馆。

  There are many forms of ancient palace construction but their complex parts are in both sides, thus different processing coming into being the distinct artistic forms and diverse names. The construction forms of the Ancient Building Complex in Wudang Mountains are various, covering all styles of ancient architecture which can be called as a museum of ancient palace architecture in China.

装饰精美 ◎ 皇家气派
Finely Decoration　Imperial Style

装饰艺术
Art of Decoration

金、木构件艺术
engraved art of golden and wooden components

武当山古建筑群在整体格调与制作形制上严格遵循古代宫廷法式，在木作艺术上还吸收了地处南北交界处的地域风格，除庄重之外，也多了一些趣味。最具代表性的金殿，就是由工部在北京铸就，武当山组装，结构和模式都反映了宫廷建筑的严谨风格，其工艺精湛细腻，严密规整。

The Ancient Building Complex in Wudang Mountains strictly comply with the ancient royal palace formations in overall style and constructional methods. The methods used in the carpentry absorbed the regional style of north and south intersection point which are not only gravity but also vivid. The exact masterpiece is the Golden Palace whose components are founded in Beijing and then assembled in Wudang Mountain. The structural pattern reflects the strict royal palace architectural style showing the exquisite and exact technics.

琉璃艺术
art of colored glaze

武当山建筑上的琉璃构件，釉色莹润，色彩丰富，特别是在与红墙融汇一体时，与周边环境形成了庄重华丽的对比，产生出一种独特、辉煌的艺术效果，不同的是武当山屋顶所用琉璃大多不是皇宫所用的黄色，而是根据地理环境、建筑等级的不同，用绿、黑、蓝等色，使之与自然更加和谐统一，达到了最佳的艺术效果。

The glazes on the architecture of Wudang Mountain are shiny smooth and rich colored especially blending with the vermilion walls that forms the sharp contrast to the grave magnificent surroundings which produces one kind of unique splendid artistic effects. The differences are that the glazes used in the roofs of Wudang Mountain is not golden which was usually used in royal palace. The colors used in architecture of Wudang Mountain are diverse e.g. green, black and blue according to geographical environment and constructional rank aiming to achieve the best artistic effect and be harmonious with the natural scenery.

石雕艺术
stone carving art

武当山宫观中的石雕艺术，最能体现皇家气派，其形制、材料、雕刻工艺都浸透了皇家宫殿、庙堂建筑的稳重、大气、严整等特点，而浮雕的深度及流畅的风格，又反映了典型的明代特色。

武当山古建筑群是明王朝典型的皇室家庙，尤其对龙的形象刻画的非常突出，同时还把道教的一些符号融入其中，在此不仅能感受到精美的装饰效果，而且还非常适宜人们静观欣赏，给人以无穷的回味。

The stone carving art of Taoist palaces in Wudang Mountain can be the best one to show the royal majesty. The structure, materials and carving technics are all reflecting the features of staid, grand and trim royal palaces and temples. While the carvings in high or low relief and the smooth style represent the typical characteristics in the Ming Dynasty.

The Ancient Building Complex in Wudang Mountains are the typical royal temples of the Ming Dynasty. In particular, portraying the image of dragon is extremely prominent and integrates some Taoist marks in the architecture that not only achieved the effect of delicate decoration but also provide people with a comfortable eye-sight and unforgotable impression.

古代琉璃建筑构件是中国古代劳动人民经过长期的实践，在琉璃工艺不断提高的条件下，将琉璃釉涂在坯胎上烧制的各式各样的琉璃建筑构件。从实际功用上讲，琉璃瓦不吸水，降雨后屋面的荷重不会增加，从而保证了屋顶承重的稳定性，而且涂了琉璃釉后，瓦面变得十分光洁，雨水流动通畅，大大加强了屋面排水效果，解决了漏雨问题，后来逐渐演变为封建等级高低的一个标志，琉璃构件颜色、大小的不同反映出建筑等级的高低。

The ancient glazed building components are those various glazed building components fired when the glaze is smeared upon the semi-finished product after the long-time practice of the ancient people in China under the condition of the continuous advancement of the colored glaze technology. Practically, the glazed tile does not absorb water and the supporting weight of the roof will not increase after the rain, ensuring the stability of the weight of the roof. Moreover, after the smearing of the glaze, the surface of the tile will become quite smooth, enabling the unhindered flow of the rain water and the effectiveness of the drainage on the roof which solves the problem of rain leakage. Afterwards they gradually represent the feudal class level according to the disparity of the color and size of the glazed components.

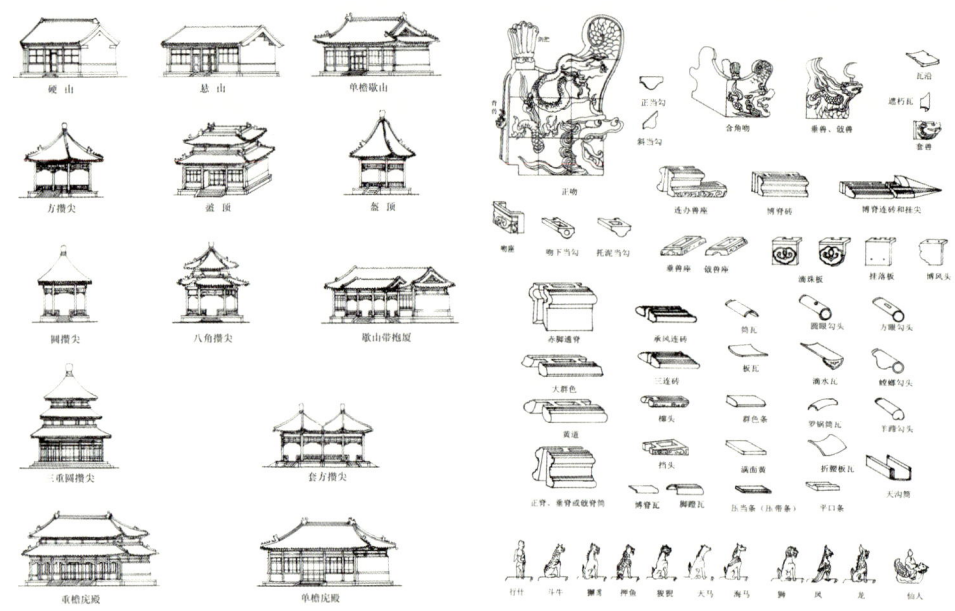

【合角吻】

合角吻安装在盝顶平台、重檐顶（如重檐庑殿、重檐歇山）第二檐以及墙脊的转角处，由两个吻兽组成，呈90度。阳角的为阳合角吻，阴角的为阴合角吻。有时两吻使用一个剑柄，有时则用两个剑柄拼成90度。合角吻的作用在于保护角柱外皮，并起装饰作用。此外，合角吻的使用受到等级限制，只有使用正吻的屋顶才有合角吻，建筑等级较低的屋顶使用望兽，转角处用合角兽，不使用合角吻。

The cornered dragon-head ridge ornament

It is installed in the corner of the wall ridge and the second eave of luding (the truncated roof) platform and multiple-eave roof (such as multiple-eave wudian and multiple-eave Chinese hip-and-gable roof), including two wenshous (dragon-head ridge ornament) arranged squarely. The external corner is the outside cornered dragon-head ridge ornament, and the internal corner is the inside cornered dragon-head ridge ornament. Sometimes the two share one sword handle, but sometimes they use their own sword handle which are arranged squarely. The usage of the cornered dragon-head ridge ornament is for the protection of the corner post's outside skin and for decoration. Furthermore, it is limited by the class. Only the roof having a zhengwen (dragon-head main ridge ornament) could use the cornered dragon-head ridge ornament. If the roof belongs to the lower class, it will use wangshou (the roof dragon-head animal ornament), the corner decorated with the cornered dragon-head animal ornament, not the cornered dragon-head ridge ornament.

【玛瑙柱】

玛瑙柱用于琉璃须弥座束腰拐角部位，主要起装饰作用。

The agate post

It is installed in the corner of shuyao of the glazed pedestal for decoration.

【额枋】

额枋是两柱之间起联系作用的横木断面，一般为矩形，宋朝时称为阑额，是柱上用于联系、承重的水平构件。南北朝之前多置于柱顶，隋唐后才移到柱间。有时两根叠用，上层额枋清朝称为大额枋，下面的叫小额枋。

Efang (the decorated tie-beam)

It is the horizontal timber section between two posts for connection. It is usually a rectangle, called lan'e in the Song Dynasty, the horizontal component on the post for connection and weight support. Before the Northern and Southern Dynasty, it was mostly installed on top of the post, while after the Sui Dynasty and the Tang Dynasty, it was removed to the space between two posts. Sometimes two efang are used together, the upper one called big efang in the Qing Dynasty, the lower one called small efang.

【屋面檐头组合】

屋面檐头组合主要是指大木建筑斗栱以上的挑檐的檩、檐、飞椽、两层望板、闸档板、瓦口、勾头、滴水等部分的组合。

The roofing eave series

It mainly refers to the projecting eave purlin, eave, flying-rafter, two-story roof boarding, sluice gate sheeting, tile opening, goutou (eaves tile), and drip channel etc. above dougong (the corbel bracket) of the heavy timber construction.

【套兽】

套兽是中国古代建筑屋面上使用的脊兽之一，安装于仔角梁的端头上，主要是防止屋檐角遭到雨水侵蚀。套兽一般由琉璃瓦制成，多为狮子头或者龙头形状。

Taoshou

It is one of jishou in ancient Chinese architecture, installed at the end of the corner balk for the prevention of the eroding of the eave corner by rain. It is commonly made of glazed tiles, shaped like a lion's head or a dragon's.

【背兽】

背兽是古代建筑屋面上的装饰构件，多用于正吻尾部。

Beishou

It is a decorative component at the end of zhengwen (the dragon-head main ridge ornament) on the roof of the ancient building.

【垫栱板】

垫栱板是连接两斗栱之间的建筑构件。

Diangongban (the pad arch board)

It is a component linking two dougong(corbel brackets).

【垫枋】

垫枋是古建筑中调节额枋连系作用的构件。

Dianfang (the pad purlin)

It is a component adjusting the connection among efang in the ancient architecture

【垂兽、戗兽】

垂兽、戗兽都是中国古代建筑的装饰性构件(早期还具有一定的防渗漏功能)，一般是垂脊尽头安垂兽，戗脊尽头安戗兽。戗兽样式与垂兽类似。明清时期，垂兽和戗兽都雕刻出完整的兽头，须向后卷，束起如火焰状，头下雕刻出部分鳞身。

Chuishou (the drooping-ridge mounted animal ornament) and qiangshou (the hip-mounted animal ornament)

They are both roof decorations. Normally chuishou is installed at the end of the drooping ridge and qiangshou at the end of the hip. The mode of qiangshou is the same as that of chuishou. In the Ming and Qing Dynasty, chuishou and qiangshou both had a full-carved head, with the beard back-rolled and bundled like the flame, and the imbricate body was partially carved below the head.

【正吻】

正吻又名鸱吻、螭吻，是安装于中国古代建筑屋顶正脊两端的装饰件。正吻呈龙头形，龙口大开，咬住正脊，系釉陶或琉璃制品。该正吻原安装于玉虚宫山门上，后因维修将其更换。地方建筑的正吻样式很多，相互之间风格差异也很大。正吻的形象也引出过不少趣谈。传说这种正吻是海龙王的九子之一，属水，能激浪成雨，把它放在屋脊上可以当作灭火消灾的"镇物"，但又怕它吞下整条屋脊，故用宝剑将它牢牢锁住。龙所具有的那种威武奋发、勇往直前和所向披靡、无所畏惧的精神，正是中华民族理想的象征和化身。龙文化是中华灿烂文化的重要组成部分，房脊上的龙文化，究其源可上溯至汉代。1960年，在湖北省沙市郊区发现一件筒瓦脊兽，瓦内壁刻有"元光元年"（公元前134年），距今已近2100年，这是已知现存最早的纪年脊兽。可见中国建筑上的吻兽，至迟在西汉时期就比较完备了。鸟形演变为鸱尾（传说是一种海中能灭火的神物），至中唐或晚唐出现张口吞脊的鸱吻。宋代以后龙形的吻兽增多，清时已很普遍，表面饰龙纹，四爪腾空，龙首怒目张口吞住正脊，脊上插着一柄宝剑，造型完美，称为"正吻"、"龙吻"、"大吻"。正脊以外的垂脊、戗脊上则常用兽头，这些兽头顺着脊的方向面向外望去，故名望兽。鸱吻最喜欢四处眺望，常饰于正脊上，它形似鱼尾，张牙舞爪，似乎要吞下整个屋脊，故又名"吞脊兽"。

正吻通常为龙型，兽头朝内张口衔脊相连，正吻位于正脊两端和垂脊的交汇点，正是防水的最薄弱环节，因此其作用是加固正脊，防止漏雨。正吻主要用于高等级殿堂，如宫殿、坛庙等。

The dragon-head main ridge ornament

It is also called Chiwen, a kind of decoration installed on both sides of the main ridge of the building's roof. It is shaped like a dragon's head, with the dragon's mouth wide open and biting the main ridge, having a glazed pottery or glazed texture. This one was first installed on the gate of the Yuxu Palace, and later it was replaced because of maintenance. There are various kinds of zhengwen in the local buildings, with huge differences between each other, and its image has raised many legend or anecdote. It is said that zhengwen is one of the nine sons of the sea dragon king. It belongs to the water property and it can surge the wave and produce the rain. Putting it onto the roof ridge could put out the fire and prevent disasters. However, there is still some kind of concern about its swallowing the whole roof ridge, so a sword is pricked into it tightly. The spirit in the dragon, with power, nisus, bravery, invincibility, and boldness, is just the embodiment of the ideal of the Chinese nation. The dragon culture is a significant component of the splendid Chinese culture, and the dragon culture on the roof ridge could be dated back to the Han Dynasty. In 1960, the earliest ridge animal ornament was found in the suburb area of Sha city in Hubei province. In the inner part of the tile, there is "yuanguang yuannian"(the first year of the Yuanguang's reign) carved, which means 134 B.C., about 2100 years before present. So we can see that wenshou (the dragon-head ridge ornament) appeared in the Chinese architecture is relatively mature in the Western Han Dynasty at latest. The shape of bird evolved into chiwei (a sacred object which could put out the fire under the sea). And until the mid-Tang or late-Tang Dynasty, chiwen made its presence, having its mouth wide open and biting the ridge. After the Song Dynasty, the dragon-shaped wenshou has increased its number, and it was already very common in the Qing Dynasty. On the surface, there carves a dragon with its claws all in the air. It glowers and bites the main ridge on which pricks a sword, forming a perfect artistic image. It was called "zhengwen", "longwen", or "dawen". The animal heads are usually used on the drooping ridge and hip except the main ridge. Those heads are watching outside in the same direction as the ridge, and then so it called "wangshou". Chiwen likes looking all around, usually installed on the main ridge. It has a fishtail shape, saber rattling, seeming to swallow the whole ridge of the house up, so it is also called "tunjishou".

The main ridge is usually in the shape of a dragon, with head turning inward and its mouth biting the ridge, and its back is linked with the ridge of the house by nails. The main ridge situates in the intersection between the both sides of the main ridge and the drooping ridge which is the weakest part in water proofing. Therefore, it is used for reinforcing the main ridge and preventing rain leakage. It is mainly applied in the high-class hall, such as palace, temple and so on.

【琉璃排山构件】

琉璃排山构件是歇山或硬山建筑两山墙屋面与垂脊之间的过渡构件。

The glazed gable framework components

They are the transitional components between the roof and the drooping ridge of xieshan and yingshan building.

【仙人走兽】

仙人走兽分仙人和走兽两部分,其数量和宫殿的等级相关,最高为11个,每个走兽都有自己的名字和作用。

仙人走兽最早出现于汉朝的明器上,开始并没有固定的使用规则,元朝以前多为武将所用,后逐渐形成定制。位于最前端的是仙人,即仙人骑凤,后面是走兽,通常数量为奇数,9为最高,依次是:龙、凤、狮子、天马、海马、狻猊、押鱼、獬豸、斗牛。但是在故宫的太和殿上,在斗牛之后又增加了一个行什,表示规格之高。其中龙、凤象征吉祥;狮子为镇山之王;天马、海马象征皇家威德通天入海;斗牛、押鱼可以兴云作雨,镇火防灾;狻猊则为能食虎豹的异兽,象征百兽率从;獬豸善辨是非,象征皇家的所谓"正大光明";行什似猴,为押尾兽,因排行第十,故名行什。屋脊上安装鸱吻走兽等物件作用有五:一是平衡稳定;二是装饰;三是避邪;四是防火;五是防漏雨。

Xianren zoushou (the ridge ornamentation of celestial-being and beasts)

It has two parts: xianren (the ridge-mounted celestial-being ornament) and zoushou (the ridge-mounted beast ornament). Its quantity has some relationship with the class of the palace, with the highest as 11. Every zoushou has its own name and usage.

Xianren zoushou first appeared on the burial object in the Han Dynasty. At the beginning, there was no fixed using regulation. Before the Yuan Dynasty, it is mostly the military officer, and then gradually it becomes customization. In the front is xianren, i.e. the celestial being riding on the phoenix. In the back is zoushou, usually in the odd number, with 9 as the highest, and respectively they are: dragon, phoenix, lion, heavenly steed, hippocampus, suanni (lion or wild horse), yayu, xiezhi (ancient goat reputed to gore guilty person at court), corrida. However, in the Hall of Supreme Harmony of the Summer Palace, another object is added after corrida in order to show the highest standard. Among those 9 zoushou, the dragon and phoenix represent luck; the lion is the king of the mountain; the heavenly steed and hippocampus symbolize the almightiness of the royalty; the corrida and yayu could control the cloud and rain to put out the fire and to prevent disasters; suanni is a strange beast who can eat tiger and leopard representing the obedience of all animals; xiezhi could make a clear distinction between right and wrong, representing the so-called "fairness and uprightness" of the royalty; that additional object the ending beast, is like a monkey, ranked 10. The functions of installing zoushou and other objects on the ridge of the house are for balance and stability, for decoration, for talismanic effect, for fireproofing, and for rain leakage prevention.

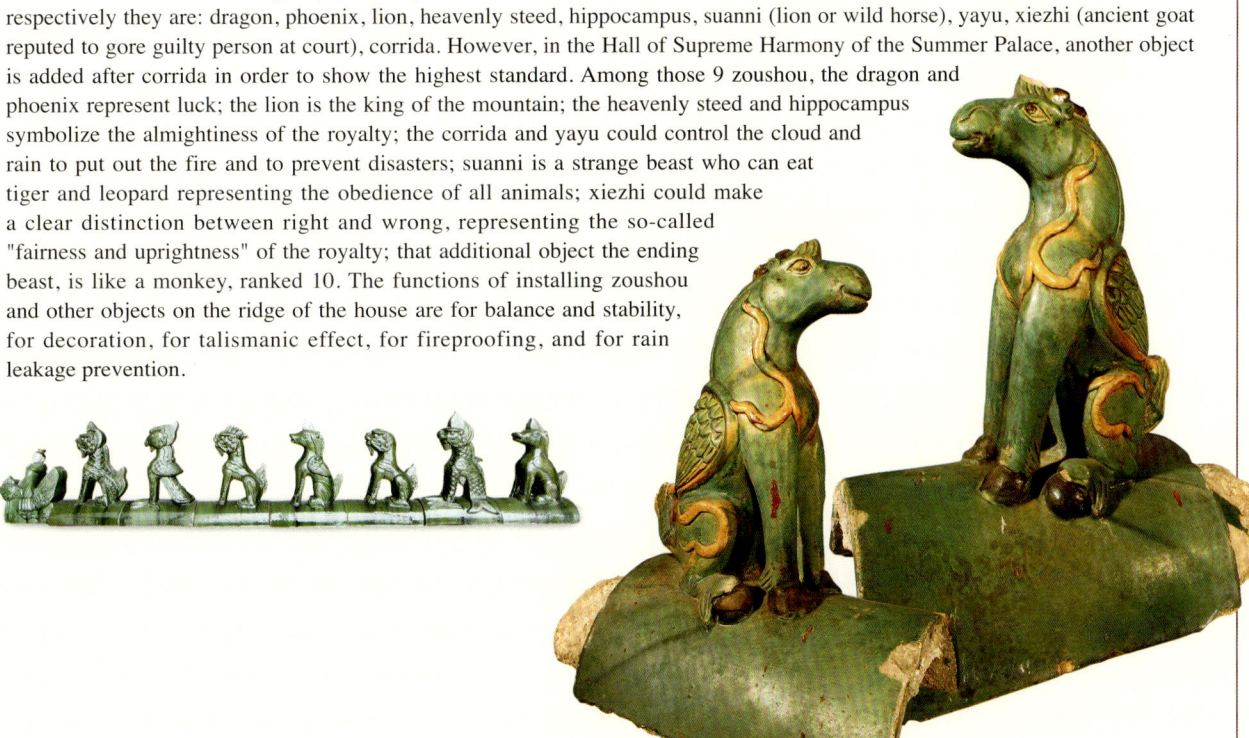

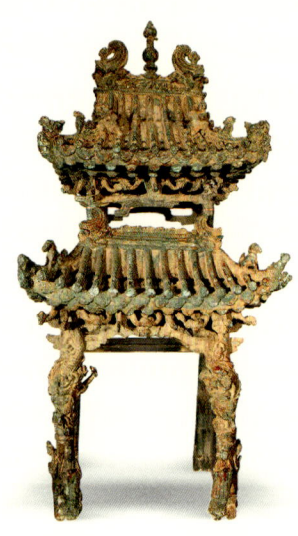

【禹迹亭】

明，铜铸鎏金，高63.4cm，宽30cm，重18.6kg。传说禹在武当山治水，因其治水有功，深受百姓的爱戴和拥护。为了纪念禹，当地百姓就在武当山紫霄宫前兴建禹迹池，以示纪念。该亭出土于紫霄宫禹迹池内，是一件金属仿大木结构重檐歇山式建筑。

The Yu Pavilion

This pavilion is copper gild, made in Ming Dynasty with the height of 63.4cm, 30cm wide and 18.6kg. It is said that Yu has succeeded in the water control in the Wudang Mountains, so he has got the public's love and support. To commemorate him, the Yu Pool was built in front of the Purple Heaven Palace in Wudang Mountain. The Yu Pavilion was unearthed from the Yu Pool in the Purple Heaven Palace, and it is a metallic wood-like multiple-eave building with some kind of xieshan building flavor.

【石雕砂岩六足器物座】

明，砂岩质地，局部有残损，原存武当山南岩宫。通高74.7cm，宽65cm，重158.8kg。雕刻手法线条流畅，造型优美，舒展大方，底足翻卷自然，为武当山现存唯一的砂岩质地石雕，主要是安放香炉之用。

The stone-carved sandrock six-leg pedestal

It is made in the Ming Dynasty, sandstone, partly lost. It was originally preserved in the South Crag Palace in the Wudang Mountains. It is 74.7cm high, 65cm wide and 158.8kg weight. It is smoothly carved, beautiful design, with its bottom feet naturally rolled which is the only stone-carved sandstone sculpture mainly for the placement of the censer.

【汉白玉石雕器物座】

汉白玉石雕器物座均为原武当山宫观内安放香炉、宝瓶等道教供器的石雕构件，由皇家御赐。器物座通饰云纹、卷草、如意、卍字图案，雕刻手法精美、细腻，均为不可多得的石雕珍品。

White marble stone-carved pedestal

They used to be the stone-carved article for the placement of censer, treasure vase, and other Taoist offering instrument in the palaces and temples in the Wudang Mountains. It was bestowed by the royalty with exquisitely and smoothly carved, being the rare and precious stone-carved cultural relic in the Wudang Mountains. It decorated with moir, Juan Cao, Ruyi and "卍"pattern.

【漆木雕金圣旨牌】

明，木质，漆雕贴金，通高129.5cm，宽113.2cm，底板厚2cm，边框厚5.8cm，重17.8kg。明永乐十一年（1413）御赐武当山，原存武当山五龙宫，为颁谕道众的禁令圣旨。此圣旨牌做工考究，工艺精湛，据故宫博物院专家朱家溍教授考证，制作此圣旨牌需工序83道。其外形为圆首，红底，边框周设九条龙纹，背面边框装饰阴线团云纹，圣旨内容与纹饰皆由漆金工艺做成，是武当山遗存的明代珍贵漆木雕文物。

The woodcarving golden imperial edict board

This board is made of wood, Ming Dynasty. It is 129.5cm high, 113.2cm wide. The baseboard is 2cm thick, for the frame is 5.8cm thick with the weight of 17.8kg.It is the royal decree of the Wudang Mountains commanded by Emperor Zhudi in the 11th year of Yongle's reign in the Ming Dynasty. It was originally preserved in Five Dargon Palace, being the interdictory royal decree to the public. With its exquisite craftsmanship and through the research by Professor Zhu Jiajin of the Palace Museum, there are 83 working procedures for this board's production. It is with a round head, red background, nine-dragon decoration on the frame, and the shade-line clouded decoration over the frame in the back. The content of the imperial edict and the veined ornament are all made through the gilded craftsmanship. And this woodcarving golden imperial edict board is a precious cultural relic in the Ming Dynasty preserved in the Wudang Mountains.

【琉璃岔角】

琉璃岔角多用于照壁壁心四角，均为三角形，主要起装饰作用。

The glazed chajiao

It mostly used in the four corners in the center of the screen wall, all triangle shaped, for decoration.

【琉璃裙板】

琉璃裙板为琉璃照壁下端的组成部分。

The glazed apron board

It is the component of the lower part of the glazed screen wall.

【琉璃隔扇门】

琉璃隔扇门又名格子门，是指安装在门槛框内的活动性屏障门，行人出入时既可开关，特殊情况下又可灵活装拆。隔扇门由外框、心屉、裙板等组成。这组琉璃隔扇门为焚帛炉等小品建筑上所使用的外墙面装饰，此门只为装饰门，不能开启。

The glazed partition board

It also called the grid door, is the flexible barrier door installed in the frame of the threshold. It can be turned on and off when there are people coming in and out, and under special situation, it can be flexibly installed and uninstalled. The partition door is composed of the outer frame, the center drawer, and the apron board. This group of glazed partition boards is the decoration for the outer wall of the silk-burning furnace, only for the purpose of decoration, unable to be turned on and off.

【莲花状建筑构件】

莲花状建筑构件出土于武当山遇真宫西宫,为明早期建筑装饰构件,多用于建筑宝顶或塔刹之上。

The lotus-like building components

They are unearthed from the Yuzhen Palace in the Wudang Mountain, belonging to the decorative building components in the early Ming Dynasty, usually used on the top of tower

【砖雕走兽】

砖雕走兽与前面所见的琉璃仙人走兽在功能上是一样的,只是质地不同而已。该组走兽为陶土烧制。

The brick-carving zoushou

It has the same function as the glazed xianren zoushou seen before, only different at the texture, being made of pottery clay.

【鱼壳瓦】

鱼壳瓦是坐放在屋面正脊下面的内装专用瓦件,主要是用来防雨,清朝以后,这种做法已基本消失。该组鱼壳瓦出土于玉虚宫。

The fish-shell tile

It is the inner-installed special tile under the main ridge of the roof for the waterproof purpose. After the Qing Dynasty, this kind of usage has basically disappeared. This fish-shell tile comes from Yuxu Palace.

【铭文砖】

该铭文砖为原武当山周府庵所用，砖上有"苏州内阁申府"、"周府"字样。

The inscription brick

It was originally used in the Zhoufu'an in the Wudang Mountains. The inscription on the brick mainly records the using place of the brick.

【束腰】

束腰是建筑中须弥座的座中构件。束腰的表面均要雕刻花纹，其式样为多种样式的"椀花结带"。对于较高等级的束腰，一般要在转角处使用角柱石，角柱石通称为"金刚柱"，一般雕刻有如意花形等。

Shuyao

It is one of the components of xumi pedestal in architecture. On the surface of shuyao carves some patterns of diversified forms of "Wan flower strips with knots". For those relatively-high level shuyao, the corner-post stone should be used in the corner. The corner-post stone is commonly called "diamond post", usually with glaze carving or ruyi shape and so on.

【石雕舞神】

元,石质,残,通高34.5cm,残宽44.6cm,重23.7kg。原存武当山隐仙岩,头部佚失。刻像身着胡服,脚穿胡靴,线条简洁流畅,舞姿优美。其雕刻手法古朴、娴熟,线条圆润,且奏且舞,裙带飘逸,显得特别自然、生动。

The stone-carved dancing god

It is made in the Yuan Dynasty, stone, partly lost. It is 34.5cm high, 44.6cm wide of the damaged part and 23.7kg weight. It was originally preserved on the Yinxian Rock in the Wudang Mountains, with its head lost. Although it is of simple line, from its dancing gesture, clothes, and boots, the carving technique reveals its adeptness. It seems to dance, and at the same time to play the musical instrument, its waistband elegantly swinging, natural and vivid.

【石雕飞天】

唐,石质,残,通高16.9cm,残宽49.5cm,重10.2kg。该石雕飞天原存武当山隐仙岩,头部佚失,双手托物,昂首挺胸,双腿后扬,衣裙巾带随风舒展。其雕刻手法采用了较娴熟的圆刀刻法,衣纹自然流畅,人体比例刻画准确,线描流畅有力,为石雕中不可多得的珍品,对研究武当道教的历史、文化具有很高的价值。

The stone-carved feitian (flying apsaras)

It is made in the Tang Dynasty, stone, partly lost. It is 16.9cm height, 49.5cm wide and 10.2kg. It was originally preserved on the Yin Xian Rock in the Wudang Mountains, with its head lost holding something in hands with head holding high. It has adopted the skilled round-carving technique, making the clothes lines natural and smooth. It is a rare precious one among the stone-carved articles, providing a quite high value for the research on the history and culture of the Taoism in the Wudang Mountains.

【汉白玉石雕构件】

该汉白玉石雕构件为武当山遇真宫张三丰坐像龙椅残件，其上满雕腾龙、云纹图案，雕刻手法细腻、生动，做工精良。

The white marble stone-carved articles

This one comes from Yu Zhen Palace, a part from the chair which Zhang Sanfeng sit. The pattern is about dargon and clound with exquisite and vivid carving technique, and with a polish work.

原武当山周府庵照壁
Wall Screening of Former Zhou Fu Hut in Wudang Mountain

【铁望柱】

望柱是指用于月台周围和桥梁两侧栏板之间的立柱，又称栏杆柱，一般多为石质、木质。该铁望柱是武当山现存唯一的金属质地望柱，通高78cm，直径10cm，重31.6kg。柱体表面阳铸有"万历四十三年二月吉日，唐府谨施，皇帝万万岁"字样，对研究武当山古代建筑以及民间玄天上帝信仰都是不可多得的实物例证。

The iron baluster column

The baluster column is the upright stanchion between the ambience of the platform and the fence board on the two sides of the bridge, which is also called banister, mostly stone-made or wood-made. This iron baluster column is the only metal baluster column in the Wudang Mountains till now as well with the height of 78cm, diameter of 10cm and 31.6kg. On the surface, there are text telling the making time and the person who made it. This is the very precious real example for the research on the ancient buildings in the Wudang Mountains and the belief in Xuan Tian God.

【抱鼓石】

抱鼓石又名"戗鼓"，是指桥面或台阶两端栏杆尽头（或起步的第一块石栏）的栏板石。一般将石面雕刻成圆鼓形花纹，故也称为抱鼓石。有些做法非常讲究，常雕刻成麒麟、坐龙、狮子、狻猊等状，统称为靠山兽或靠山狮子、靠山麒麟等。该抱鼓石长143cm，厚16.5cm，重185kg，其上除了雕刻有降龙图案外，还刻意雕刻了一头大象，并且使用了夸张的手法将大象的鼻子卷成石鼓形，形象十分可爱，是武当山现存的珍贵石雕精品。

Baogushi (the drum-shaped stone block)

It is also called "qianggu", the fence board stone at the end of the banisters on the two sides of the bridge or the steps (or the first stone banister). The surface of the stone block is usually carved with drum patterns, so it also named "baogushi (the drum-shaped stone block)". Some are done so daintily, having the shape like the kylin, sitting dragon, lion, suanni (lion or wild horse), and so on which are called by a joint name, the mountain animal or the mountain lion, the mountain kylin, and so on. This one is 143cm long, 16.5cm thick and 185kg weight. Apart from the falling-dragon pattern, an elephant pattern is also deliberately carved on it, and the tongue (or nose) of the elephant is exaggerated to be rolled like a drum. The image is very lovely. It could be regarded as one of the exquisite articles in sculpture.

【石雕升降龙照壁盒子】

石雕升降龙照壁盒子由两部分组成，均为半圆形，直径159.5cm，厚17cm，重600kg，原为武当山周府庵前照壁盒子上的装饰物，它和照壁上的岔角是体现照壁艺术性高低的最主要部位。盒子和岔角的图案题材丰富、花样繁多，有花草、山水、走兽、飞禽、龙凤等。琉璃照壁面采用不同的图案，形成不同的风格。因此，盒子和岔角的雕琢艺术，就成了衡量一座照壁艺术价值高低的最重要标志。该照壁盒子上雕刻着一条升龙和一条降龙，组成了一组二龙戏珠图案，雕刻极为精美，具有很高的艺术价值。

The stone-carved screen-wall box with the rising and falling dragon pattern

It is consist of two parts. Both are semicircular one, the diameter is 159.5cm and 17cm thick, 600kg weight. It is originally the decoration on the screen-wall box in front of the Zhoufu'an in the Wudang Mountains. It, together with the chajiao on the screen wall, is the main part to judge the level of the screen wall's artistic quality. The pattern of the box and chajiao has a wide range of themes and various designs, such as flowers and grass, mountains and water, animals, fowls, dragons and phoenixes. The surface of the glazed screen wall adopts a variety of patterns, forming diversified styles. Therefore, the carving art of the box and chajiao becomes the most important sign to decide the value of the screen wall. On the screen wall box, there are a rising dragon and a falling dragon, forming the pattern of two dragons playing with a bead. The carving is so exquisite that the box has a very high artistic value.

【斗栱】

斗栱是中国古代大木建筑的重要结构部件，依据所在位置有不同的名称。在柱头之上的斗栱称为柱头科，在柱间额枋上的斗栱称为平身科，在屋角柱头之上的斗栱称为角科。这里展示的六组斗栱分别是仿照明代武当山金殿及玉虚宫嘉靖御碑亭的做法按比例制作。斗栱一般使用在高等级的官式建筑中，大体分为外檐斗栱和内檐斗栱。斗栱踩数均为奇数，如三踩、五踩、七踩、九踩、十一踩等，踩数愈多等级愈高。

斗栱在结构上挑出以承重，并将屋檐的荷载经斗栱传递到柱上。它又有一定的装饰作用，从唐到清，斗栱的结构作用越来越小，装饰性越来越强，斗栱的排布由疏到密，由大变小。斗栱是封建礼制的重要体现，等级森严，同时也是建筑尺度的标准。

Dougong (the corbel bracket)

It is one of the building components in the heavy timber construction in the ancient China. The dougong on the column head belongs to the column-top corbel bracket set, the one on the efang between columns belongs to the intermediate corbel-bracket set, and the one on the column head in the corner of the house belongs to the corner corbel-bracket set. These six groups of dougong displayed here are respectively made proportionally by imitating the making way of the Golden Palace and the Jiajing Yubei Pavilion in the Yuxu Palace of Ming Dynasty. Dougong is commonly used in the high-class official-type buildings, generally including the outer-eaves corbel bracket and the inner-eaves corbel bracket. The number of cai of dougong is odd, like three cai, five cai, seven cai, nine cai, eleven cai, and so on. The more the cai, the higher the class.

With regard to the structure, dougong projects for weight supporting, and transfers the supporting weight of the eave to the column through itself. It also has a decorative function. From the Tang Dynasty to the Qing Dynasty, the structural function of dougong has decreased, while its decorative function has increased. The distribution of dougong is from sparse to dense and from big to small. Dougong is a significant representation of the ritual system, with strict classification, and the standard for determining the building scale as well.

斗栱模型　Dougong

【石雕托塔力士像】

该四尊石雕托塔力士像均通高76cm，宽40cm，厚40cm，重145kg，是武当山古建筑群中现存唯一的佛教墓塔上的沙弥力士像。佛塔为明万历三十年（1602），皇帝派遣太监黄勋等祭祀"不二和尚"圆信所修建，现存于武当山展旗峰后。由于此塔坐落于武当山道教建筑群中，且又在武当道教鼎盛时期所兴建，它的存在不能不说是一个奇迹，可以说它也是武当山佛、道融合的历史见证。

stone-carved strong men's statues holding the tower up

Each of the statues is 76cm high, 40cm wide and 40cm thick with the weight of 145kg. They are the only stone-carved strong men statues holding the tower up on the Buddhist tomb tower in the ancient building complex in the Wudang Mountains. They are made in the 30th year of Wanli reign of Ming Dynasty. They are originally preserved behind the Flying Flag Peak, among the Taoist building complex and built in the prosperity period of Taoism. Its survival could be miracle, so we can say that it is the historical evidence for the combination of Buddhism and Taoism in the Wudang Mountains.

"不二"塔　Bu'er Tower

【雀替】

雀替是中国古代建筑中非常特殊的构件之一，多安置于梁或阑额与柱交接处，是承托梁枋的木构件，可以缩短梁枋的净跨距离（也用在柱间的落挂下，但是为纯装饰性构件），增加梁头抗剪能力。清代称为雀替，又称为"插角"或"托木"、"牛腿"，安置在梁与柱交点的角落，具有稳定和装饰的功能。雀替从力学上的构件，逐渐发展成美学的构件，就像一对翅膀在柱的上部向两边伸出，生动的形式随着柱间框格而改变，轮廓由直线转变为柔和的曲线，由方形变成有趣而更为丰富、更自由的多边形。雀替有龙、凤、仙鹤、鹿、狮子、麒麟、金蟾等各种形式，雕法则有圆雕、浮雕、透雕等。建筑厅共展出木雕麒麟和木雕狮子各一对，其雕刻工艺精美，技法娴熟，是武当山明代建筑遗存的原物，为木雕中的精品之作。

Queti (the decorated bracket)

It is a special name in Chinese architecture. It is a wooden component for supporting the girder and purlin, being installed in the intersection between girder or lan'e and column, which can shorten the net span of girder and purlin. It is also used under the dropping between columns, but it is purely decorative, being able to strengthen the anti-cutting capability of the girder head or to shorten the span of girder and purlin. In the Qing Dynasty, it was called queti, chajiao, tuomu, or niutui, installed in the corner of the intersection between the girder and the purlin for stability and decoration. The gradual development of queti from the component in mechanics to that in aesthetics is just like the stretching of a pair of wings in the upper part of the column, a vivid form changing with the frame between columns, the outline from beeline to soft curve, from square to the interesting, richer, and freer polygon. Queti has a plenty of forms, like dragon, phoenix, immortal crane, deer, lion, kylin, golden cicada, and so on. The carving techniques include the circular carved work, the relief sculpture, the openwork carving, etc.. The Art of Architecture Hall display are respectively the woodcarving kylin and the woodcarving lion, with exquisite and skilled craftsmanship. They are the real objects of the remaining buildings in the Ming Dynasty in the Wudang Mountains and the exquisite ones in the woodcarving articles.

木雕麒麟　wood-carved Kylin

【铜铸鎏金武当真武修真模型】

明,铜铸鎏金,高128cm,宽63cm,重60kg。明万历44年(1616)由北京工部勘合铸造。该模型为武当山人文和自然景观的浓缩,它将金殿等建筑与祥云、古树、神仙以及真武修真故事等融于一体铸就。模型下端饰五位龙面人身像,寓五龙捧圣山之意,将武当山整体托起,布局紧凑而富于想象,是武当山馆藏文物中的精品。

The copper gilding Wudang Zhenwu's cultivating deity model

It is made in Ming Dynasty, copper gild, 128cm high, 63cm wide and 60kg weight. It was founded by the Ministry of Works in Beijing in the 44th year of the Wan Li's reign in Ming Dynasty. It concentrates the landscape of the Wudang Mountains, combing the Golden Palace and other buildings with the auspicious cloud, the ancient tree, the deity, and the story of Zhenwu's cultivating deity. Below the model, there are five statues with dragon's face and human's body, symbolizing the holding of the sacred mountain by the five dragons. The layout is so compact and imaginative. This model could be considered as an exquisite article among those cultural relics in the museum in the Wudang Mountains.

【"治世玄岳"石牌坊】

"治世玄岳"石牌坊亦称"玄岳门",位于武当山东麓,是古代进入武当山的大门。玄岳门建于明嘉靖三十一年(1552),是一座四柱三间五楼式石牌坊,面阔14.5米,通高11.9米,柱下有覆盆式柱顶石,柱周设有夹杆石以铁箍加固。中柱上架龙门坊,坊下为透雕腾龙翔鹤瑞云花板。花板中间有嘉靖皇帝亲笔题写的"治世玄岳"四个大字。下额枋下为高浮雕瑞鹤呈祥花板,花板下以龙鱼雀替承托,以缩小花板的跨度,减轻额枋上层的重量。次间柱上、中枋之间为透雕缠枝花草和双凤花板。边楼也通体刻有仙鹤流云图案,中枋、下枋之间花板为高浮雕瑞鹤呈祥。主楼为庑殿式,宝瓶吞口,花板正脊,大吻对峙,出七踩双翘偷心造斗栱。次楼、边楼脊饰与主楼相似,自上而下,逐层设置,形成三滴水式的格局。中柱两边各出有三个单翘,边柱各出有一个单翘,翘上嵌有圆雕八仙和封神人物。

牌坊结构简练,造型雄伟,较为严格地仿照了木构牌楼的做法。坊身通体雕刻,装饰华丽,制作精细,特别是运用线刻、圆雕、浮雕和透雕等技法,雕刻有鸱吻、腾龙、仙鹤、瑞云、水浪、卷草、八仙和封神人物等纹饰,一反官式建筑中以龙凤狮子为主的御用纹饰,充满了神仙之气,是难得的明代石雕精品,具有很高的科学、历史、艺术价值。1988年被国务院公布为全国第三批重点文物保护单位。

"Zhishi Xuan Yue" Stone Torii

It is also named Xuan Yue Gate, located in the east of Wudang Mountain. It was built in the 31st year of Jiajing's reign in the Ming Dynasty (1552 AD). The torii is a three-room four-column five-stage building with 14.5meters wide and 11.9meters height. There are pedestal boulders of Fupen style consolidated by iron hoop around. There are Longmen lanes supported by the center pillar underneath is the card decorated with flying dragon, flying crane and the auspicious clouds. In the middle of the card, there are four Chinese characters "Zhishi Xuan Yue" which is written by Emperor Jiajing in person.

The torii has a simple structure but grand sculpt. It is fully applying the through-carved work, the circular carved work, the relief sculpture, the basso-relief work, and other techniques. The pattern has Chiwen, flying dragon, crane, cloud, water wave, and the eight immortals and other which are all so lifelike, with exquisite craftsmanship and high scientific, historic, and artistic value. In 1988, it was classified as the third group of national key cultural relic protection unit by the State Council.

【三十万军民大修武当场景】

The scene of 300 thousand persons construct Wudang on a large scale

补秦皇汉武之遗，历朝罕见；张金阙琳宫之胜，寰宇所无。

the complement for the heritage of the emperors in the Qin and Han Dynasty, rarely seen in the history, and the expansion of the magnificence of those golden palaces, unprecedented in the universe

　　三十万军民大修武当场景为明永乐皇帝御赐营建武当道场之情景再现。明永乐十年（1412），永乐皇帝朱棣敕命隆平侯张信、驸马都尉沐昕、工部侍郎郭琎、礼部尚书金纯等军政官员等五百余人，率军民工匠三十万人，历十二年，共建成九宫、八观、三十六庵堂、七十二岩庙等三十三组建筑群，宫观庙宇多达二万余间，以及二十多座亭台，四十多座桥梁，铺筑长达一百四十华里的青石古神道，建筑面积达一百六十余万平方米。明代文人描绘为"补秦皇汉武之遗，历朝罕见；张金阙琳宫之胜，寰宇所无"，正反映出武当山古建筑群举世无双的建设规模和高超的建筑艺术。

　　This scene displays that in the 10th year of Yongle's reign, i.e. in the year of 1412, the Emperor Yongle in the Ming Dynasty commanded to construct the Wudang Taoist rites. This scene reflects the real site of building architectures in Wudang Mountain at that time. The Yongle Emperor commanded Long Pinghou, Zhang Xin, his son in law Mu Xin, Guo Jin, officer from the ministry of works, and the director of the Ministry of Rite, Jin Chun, and other military officials for around 500, together with 300,000 soldiers, civilians and craftsmen constructed Wudang on a large scale. Over twelve years, Wudang Mountain has been built thirty-three architecture complexes including 9 palaces, 8 temples, 36 ancestral temples, 72 rock temples. There are more than 20,000 temples and palaces, more than 20 pavilions, and 40 bridges or more. The ancient bluestone road is more than 100 huali, and the building area is 1,600,000 square meters or more. The scholars in the Ming Dynasty described it as "the complement for the heritage of the emperors in the Qin and Han Dynasty, rarely seen in the history, and the expansion of the magnificence of those golden palaces, unprecedented in the universe". And this reflects that the ancient building complex in the Wudang Mountains possesses the unparalleled building scale and the lofty architectural art.

建筑艺术厅一角
Sight of the Art of Architecture Hall

建筑艺术厅前言
The preface of the Art of Architecture Hall

建筑艺术厅一角
Sight of the Art of Architecture Hall

斗栱模型
model of Dougong

建筑艺术厅 Art of Architecture Hall

　　我国伟大的先民创造了灿烂的古代文化，武当山古建筑群便是这优秀文化的杰出代表。武当山现存古建筑在布局、规制、风格、材料、工艺等方面都保存了历史的原状。宫观建筑自成体系，在建筑艺术、建筑美学上均达到了极为完美的境界，蕴涵着丰富的文化和科技内涵。本展厅由于空间有限，不能向游客详尽展示，只待游客亲身到武当山去慢慢欣赏，细细品味。

　　The Chinese people created splendid ancient culture and the Ancient Building Complex in Wudang Mountains are the masterpiece of the excellent culture. The existent ancient buildings in Wudang Mountain are still maintain their original state in layout, style, material, technique etc. The architecture of temples and palaces have their own units, which are nearly perfect in art and aesthetics of architecture, and possess rich cultural and technical connotation. Due to the limited exhibition in the hall, the architecture in Wudang Mountain can not be shown to the visitors in detail which could only for visitors themselves to appreciate and taste in the Mountain.

木雕狮、麒麟　Wood-carved lion and kylin

建筑艺术厅一角　Sight of the Art of Architecture Hall

仙山名士·灵通天下

Fairy Mountain and Celebrity Famed to the World

仙山名人厅
Mountain with Celebrities Hall

"山不在高，有仙则灵"。春秋以来，从道家始祖老庄，到唐宗明祖历代帝王，以及孙思邈、吕洞宾、陈抟、张三丰、徐霞客，众多贤哲的名字与武当联系在一起，寻求"道法自然、天人合一"的朴素追求。在仙山名人展厅，观众通过丰富的展览内容，实现与历代武当仙人名士的精神对话。

A mountain needn't be high, it is famous so long as there is a deity on it. Since the Spring and Autumn Period, from the Taoist Creator to the emperors of different dynasties and also the celebrities such as Sun Simiao, Lv Dongbin, Chen Tuan, Zhang Sanfeng and Xu Xiake, they all link with Wudang Mountain to pursue that everything should follow the nature and heaven and human are united one. In this hall, you can have a spiritual conversation with the celestial beings.

历代仙真与武当山
Immortals with Wudang Mountain

历代仙真
Immortals

【老子】

老子，姓李，名耳，字聃，楚国苦县人（今河南鹿邑东），春秋晚期杰出的思想家，道家创始人。道教将他神化，奉为祖师，称为"太上老君"。老子所著《道德经》为道家的重要经典。《道德经》继承了中国古代巫史文化，特别是《易经》、《尚书》等思想并吸收了各地文化传统而写成，是一部以"道"为中心的，包括宇宙论、本体论、认识论、方法论、朴素辩证法的哲学体系。文分上下两篇，共五千余字。老子学说对中国哲学发展有很大的影响，后世很多哲学家都多角度吸收了他的思想。

Lao-tzu

Lao-tzu, whose family name was Li and surname was Er, was a Taoist master. His hometown was in the kingdom of Chu. He was a renowned philosopher in the Epoch of Spring and Autumn. He was the founder of Taoism. And the Taoism takes him as an important deity named Tai Shang Lao Jun and his *Tao Te Ching (Five-thousand Words)* was the important Taoist classical works. *Tao Te Ching* inherits the ancient Chinese sorcery culture, especially the *Book of Changes* and the book *Shangshu*, which are all absorbing the traditional culture of different places. It is a book taking Tao as its centre containing the philosophy of cosmology, ontology, epistemology, methodology and simply dialectic. The *Tao Te Ching* has two parts with the text of five thousand words. The theory of Lao-tzu has a great influence to the development of Chinese philosophy. Many philosophers take his idea from different aspects.

【庄子】

庄子，战国著名思想家，道家学派的代表人物，宋国人。老子哲学思想的继承者和发展者，先秦庄子学派的创始人。后世将他和老子并称为"老庄"，他们的哲学亦称"老庄哲学"。

Zhuang-tzu

Zhuang-tzu, was a renowned philosopher of Warring States, the representative of Taoism school. His hometown was in the Kingdom of Song. He succeeded and developed Lao-tzu philosophic thinking. And he was the originator of pre-qin Zhuang-zi school of thought. Later people put Lao-tzu and him together, "Lao Zhuang", their philosophy was called "Lao Zhuang philosophy".

【夏禹】

禹是古代治水英雄。他的儿子启建立了中国第一个奴隶制国家夏。禹治水期间曾到武当山，武当山至今还存有禹迹池、禹迹亭等遗迹。

Xia Yu

Yu was the ancient hero of regulating waterways. Qi, son of yu, established the first slave country Xia dynasty in Chinese history. During that period, Yu had been to Mt. Wudang. Up to now, it preserves relic Yu Ji pond , Yu Ji pavilion etc. in Mt. Wudang.

【尹喜】

尹喜，先秦人，相传任函谷关令时曾留老子著《道德五千言》。后尹喜弃绝人事，按老子所授经法，精修至道。该图为老子传道尹喜，尹喜功成圆满，被授玉册金文，封为无上真人。武当山尹喜岩便是他当年修炼之地。

Yin Xi

Yin Xi lived in the era before the Qin Dynasty. When he was the magistrate of Hangu Pass, he invited Lao-tzu to write *Five-thousand Words (Tao Te Ching)*. Later Yin Xi lived in seclusion and cultivated himself piously according to the theory of Lao-tzu and successfully attained the perfection of Taoism. The picture shows that Lao-tzu preached to Yin Xi, and Yin Xi succeeded, gained jade-made Golden Book and conferred as Wushang Honorable Man. The Yin Xi Crag is the place where Yin Xi once cultivated himself.

【吕洞宾】

吕洞宾，唐末著名道士，号纯阳子，民间传说的八仙之一，多次来武当修炼，在武当山留有较多遗物。

Lv Dongbin

Lv Dongbin, titled as Chun Yangzi, was a famed Taoist in the late period of Tang Dynasty. He was one of the Eight Immortals and came to Wudang for cultivation many times. There are many of his things left in Wudang Mountain.

【陈抟】

陈抟（870~988），字图南，号扶摇子，生于唐末，五代至宋初著名道士。他先后在武当山玉虚岩、凌虚岩、白云岩、南岩、五龙祠、诵经台等地修道诵经，服气辟谷二十余年，梦感五气龙君传授睡功，得"五雷蛰法"，一觉能睡半月，史称"睡仙"。宋太宗赐其号希夷先生。其得道后卧书"福寿"二字，现存南岩宫皇经堂右山墙。该像便为其独创睡功修炼图。北宋端拱元年（988）十一月二十二日在华山莲花峰下坐化，死后容色如生，肢体尚温，时有五色彩云围绕于山谷中，享年118岁。

Chen Tuan

Chen Tuan, a famous Taoist, named himself Tu'nan and Fuyaozi, lived in the late Tang Dynasty, the Five Dynasties, and the early Song Dynasty (870~988 AD). He successively practiced and chanted scriptures in Yuxu Crag, Lingxu Crag, Baiyun Crag, South Crag, Five Dragon Ancestral Temple, Reading Scriptural Platform, and other places in the Wudang Mountains. He absorbed the qi and never eats the five cereals in the valley for more than 20 years, and he felt in his dream that the five-qi dragon lord was imparting the sleeping kongfu to him, so he got the "wuleizhefa". He could sleep for half a month, so he is called "the sleeping deity" in history. The Song Taizong gave him a name, Xiyixiansheng. The two characters have been preserved on the right mountain wall of Imperial Classics Hall in the South Crag Palace. The picture was his original creation of cultivation during sleeping.On November 12th in the first year of Duangong's reign in the Northern Song Dynasty (988 AD), at the age of 118, he passed away sitting under the Lotus Summit in the Mount Huashan in Shanxi, with his face color like him alive, and his body warm. Sometimes there is some colored cloud around the valley.

历代帝王与武当山
Emperors with Wudang Mountain

历代帝王
Dynasties of Emperors

【李世民】

李世民,唐朝第二位皇帝,在位期间,国泰民安,社会稳定。贞观初年,因天下大旱,派官员到全国多处名山求雨无果,后令均州太守姚简至武当山祈雨,天下普降甘露,太宗大喜之后,遂命敕建武当山五龙祠。

Li Shimin

Li Shimin was the second emperor of Tang Dynasty, during the period he reigned, the coutry proceeded peaceful, people lead a good life in a stable society. Beacause of the great drought in the first a few years of ZhenGuan, they prayed for rain in many famous mountains, but in vain. So later he ordered officials go to Mt. Wudang praying for rain, they got it. Li Shimin was very excited, and then built Five-dragon Shrine.

【赵恒】

赵恒是北宋第三位皇帝,信奉道教,将五龙祠扩建并亲颁圣旨升祠为观,使其规格得以提高。

Zhao Heng

Zhao Heng was the third emperor of Northern Song. He showed highly respect for Taoism, extended five-dragon shrine and upgraded it to be temple, thus enhanced its specification.

【忽必烈】

忽必烈，元代杰出帝王，崇奉道教，多次将武当山作为全国的灵应之地加以奉祀。元至元二十三年（1286），世祖将五龙观升为"五龙灵应宫"，延祐元年（1314），仁宗皇帝又赐额"大天乙真庆万寿宫"。

Kublai

Kublai, a excellent emperor of Yuan Dynasty, worshiped Taoism crasily, he offered sacrifices to Mt. Wudang as the efficacious place many times. In 1286, he upgraded five-dragon temple to be "five-dragon efficacious palace", in the first year of Yanyou regin (1314), Emperor Renzong titled it Datianyizhenqin Wanshou Palace.

【朱元璋】

朱元璋，明朝开国皇帝，信奉道教。他定都南京后便建真武庙致祭。洪武十八年（1385）特授武当高道丘玄清为嘉议大夫、太常寺卿，洪武二十四年（1391）又遣使召请武当高道张三丰。

Zhu Yuanzhang

Zhu Yuanzhang was the first king of Ming dynasty who worshiped Taoism. After establishing the capital city in Nanjing, he built ZhenWu Temple for offerings. In the 18th year of HongWu (1385), Wudang high preist Qiu Xuanqing was conferred JiaYiDaFu, Tai Chang Si Qing(official title).In the 24th year of HongWu (1391), he sent an envoy to summon Wudang high preist Zhang Sanfeng.

【朱棣】

朱棣，明朝第三位皇帝。在位期间实施"南修武当，北建故宫"两大工程，对武当山建设非常关心，事无巨细，亲自御批。明永乐十年（1412）派遣朝廷重臣，发三十万军民工匠大修武当山，历十二年，在武当山共建三十三座建筑单元，房屋两万余间，创造了以金殿为主的数十个世界建筑之最。

Zhu Di

Zhu Di was the third emperor of Ming dynasty, during the period he reigned, he hold two projects, built Wudang in South, constructed Imperial Palace in North. He showed extremely concern for the construction of Mt. Wudang, built 33 building units and more than 20 thousand houses in Mt. Wudang during 12 years, and created over 10 world wonder of architecture including Golden palace.

【朱厚熜】

明世宗朱厚熜一生崇信道教，祈求长生不老。他在位期间大肆扩建武当，耗银数以万计，并新建石牌坊以示国家对武当山的旌表，同时还御敕碑亭两座以彰国威。

Zhuhoucong

Zhuhoucong worshiped Taoism all his life, and prayed for immortality. During the period he reigned, he cost a lot of money on building and extending Mt. Wudang. He newly built stone memorial archway, in order to show testimonial confer for Mt. Wudang, at the same time he built two pavilions in order to enhance its national prestige.

【爱新觉罗·玄烨】

爱新觉罗·玄烨是中国历史上在位时间最长的一位皇帝，政绩显赫。他在位期间非常重视武当山的建设，屡派重臣致祭真武，仅康熙四十二年（1703）就御笔亲书匾额五通，遣使悬挂于武当宫观。今武当山太和宫金殿内的"金光妙相"匾额就是其亲笔所书。

Kanghsi

Kanghsi was the emperor who reigned the longest period in Chinese history and who had prominent talent for politics and military. He attached great importance to the construction of Wudang Mountain and dispatched qualified officials to conduct offerings to Emperor Zhen Wu. Only in the 42nd year of Kanghsi reign (1703), he wrote five tablets and hang on palaces and temples in Wudang Mountain. The tablet written the four Chinese characters "Jin Guang Miao Xiang" in the Golden Palace is the objective illustration.

古代名人与武当山
Ancient Celebrities with Wudang Mountain

历史文物
Historical Cultural Relics

【陈抟石雕坐像】

坐像头戴五梁冠，身着官服，仪态端庄，线条自然流畅，比例准确，面部传神，是武当山遗存的宋代石刻艺术精品之一。

The stone-carved statue of Chen Tuan

The statue wear the wuliang cap and the official costume, noble, smooth, proportional with vivid facial expression. It is one of the stone-carved exquisite articles of Song Dynasty remaining in the Wudang Mountains.

【卧"福"睡"寿"】

陈抟在武当山修炼期间，梦感五气龙君传授睡功，得"五雷蛰法"。陈抟不仅在道学上有较高的造诣，而且在书法上也颇有功底，尤擅行书，大气厚重，雄浑有力。他在武当山修炼期间所书写的"福"、"寿"二字，刚柔并济，为后世文人所瞠目，至今仍存于南岩宫皇经堂墙壁之上。

The lying "fu" and the sleeping "shou" of Chen Tuan

When Chen Tuan was practicing in the Wudang Mountains, he felt in his dream that the five-qi dragon lord was imparting the sleeping kungfu to him, so he got the "wuleizhefa". Chen Tuan has reached a lot of achievement not only in the Taoist study but also in the calligraphy. The two words written by him when he was practicing in the Wudang Mountains, "fu"and "shou", have both the strong and soft features, leaving an astonishing effect on later scholars, still remaining on the wall of the Huangjing Hall of the South Crag Palace.

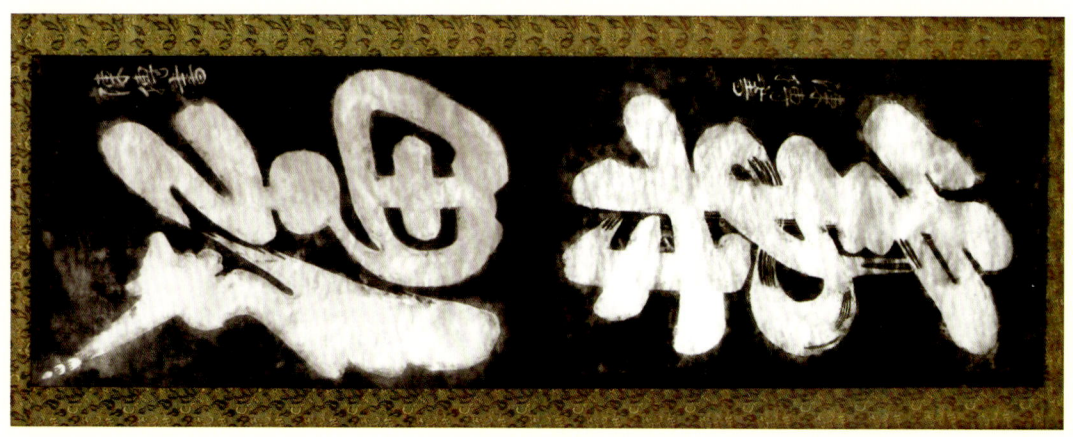

【"治世玄岳"石牌坊】

嘉靖皇帝是继明永乐皇帝之后再次大修武当山的皇帝。他笃信道教，曾为政20多年而不理朝政，专求长生，尤其推崇武当真武神。明嘉靖三十一年，亲拨帑银11万两，遣工部侍郎陆杰等率军民夫匠重修武当宫观，并敕建石牌坊一座，竣工后赐额"治世玄岳"四个大字，以示国家旌表。

"Zhishi Xuanyue" Stone Torii

Emperor Jiajing is the second emperor who construct Wudang on a large scale after Emperor Yongle. He believes in Taoism and for more than 20 years, he just cultivated for longevity and did nothing for his country's affairs. In the 31st year of Jiajing's reign in the Ming Dynasty, he send an official of the Ministry of Works came to Wudang building temples and palaces and especially asked to build this Torii. After this Torii finished, the emperor write the name of "Zhishi Xuanyue" in person.

【武当印章】

武当名类印章留存数量较多，其内容丰富，字体多样，变化有序，有大篆、小篆、楷书、金文、行书等，也有道教专用字体和云篆、龙章凤文等。篆刻内容有地名、人名、建筑名、药品、诗句、图案等，还有用于书信的封缄。另外还有一些独具特色的象形文字，种类繁多，书篆精美。

The Wudang Seal

The Wudang Seal possesses the traditional craftsmanship, with rich contents, diversified fonts, and ordered changes, including the ancient seal character, Hsiao Chuan (the lesser seal style Chinese character), the regular script, the bronze inscription, the cursive script, etc., as well as the special font used by Taoism, the cloud seal character, the dragon stamp and the phoenix text, and so on. The contents of the seal cutting include the name for place, people, and building, medicine, poem, pattern, etc., and the sealing device for letters or personal letters. There are some other pictographs with unique features which are so astonishing.

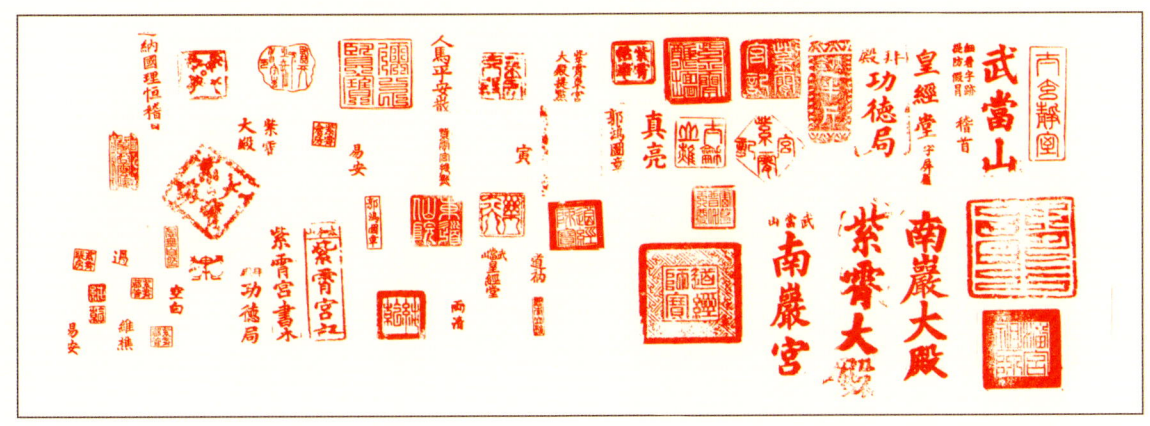

【金龙、玉璧、山简】

　　金龙、玉璧、山简为一套，1982年出土于武当山紫霄宫赐剑台。山简铭文记述了建文元年上元节（元宵节），湘献王朱柏（朱元璋第十二子）到武当山紫霄宫福地殿设立罗天大醮时而投放通神之物，即金龙、玉璧、山简。其方法是将金龙负山简、玉璧随行投入十三个不同的方位，因玉能通天神，其目的是想通过这三件宝物向上天传达平安的信号，希望能得到真武神的翊佑。然而，事情并不像想象的那样顺利，在醮事后仅几个月，迫于建文皇帝的"削藩"压力，因其惧怕治罪，在封地自焚身亡，成为皇权斗争的牺牲品。

　　金龙，长11.32cm、宽4.5cm、重15g。整条龙由两部分组成，呈昂首腾飞状，整体鳞纹丝丝入扣，清晰可辨。

　　玉璧，直径8.06cm、厚0.2cm、内圆直径1.22cm、重58g。正面为圆形，中心有一圆孔。玉璧整体呈淡绿色，表面光滑圆润、明亮细腻。

　　山简，即湘王建醮碑，为竖式长方形，抹肩，青砂岩质地，通高28.5cm、宽7.2cm、厚0.7cm、重501.5g。山简阳面刻有符咒一道，为湘王祈福之语。阴面竖刻八列，共150字。

　　碑文曰："今谨有上清大洞玄都三景弟子湘王，以今上元令节开建太晖观、太晖三景灵坛，启修太上洞玄灵宝崇真演教，福国裕民，济生渡死，普天大斋，计一千二百分，通五昼宵，今则行道事，竟投简灵山，愿神愿仙，长生渡世，飞行上清，五岳真人，至圣至灵，乞削罪录，上名九天，请旨灵山，金龙驿传。建文元年（1399）岁次乙卯正月壬申朔十五日丙戌，上清大洞经法师臣周思礼于武当山福地告闻。"

　　阴面竖式阴刻一行，文为山简符咒语。

　　根据简文得知，湘献王朱柏为"福国裕民，济生渡世"，于建文元年（1399）正月十五日在武当山紫霄宫福地殿设立了罗天大醮，由太晖观经策法师周思礼主持，按等级设斋位一千二百分，经五天五夜后又选吉时投关，宣告醮事结束。

　　按《道藏灵宝无量度人上经大法》述，投简有三种方式，即用山、水、土三简的任意一种，投向灵山、灵水、灵地。山简配用青色玉璧，为圆形；水简配用灰色玉璧，为圆八角形；土简配用白色玉璧，为四方形。取任意一种即可，投简前用梓木，长一尺二寸，宽三寸，厚三分，白粉涂简，雌黄界边，朱书符墨书诰山简。水简封皮用青纸，朱书。土简以黄纸，朱书。投简用金龙一条，金纽十二枚，玉璧一枚，事散，坛逐处设醮投之；或者用金龙十三枚，十方镇十枚，三枚随简投之。天子、皇后、太子用上金，三品以下用中金，九品以下用次金，士庶以银涂金，长三寸六分。由此而知，在武当山紫霄宫的四方四维的某十处仍有十二枚金纽。因为它随简投下的只有一条金龙，而出土地的三层叠棺与此醮事无什么干系，纯属阴阳先生选择风水之偶然巧合。因为龙在古代被人们视为"四灵"，在此意为天上的驿骑，传达通感，龙骑为先，"负简即腾信三宫，镇坛以通诚，十极镇"。另外，龙也可以在阴曹地府中传信，以避不测之祸，传说地狱中有苦差、苦刑等，通过斋醮可贿赂阎王，为其赎罪，可免于一切灾难，这是人间对死者来世一种美好愿望的寄托。古代的简一般用梓木做成，该山简则是用青砂岩磨制而成。

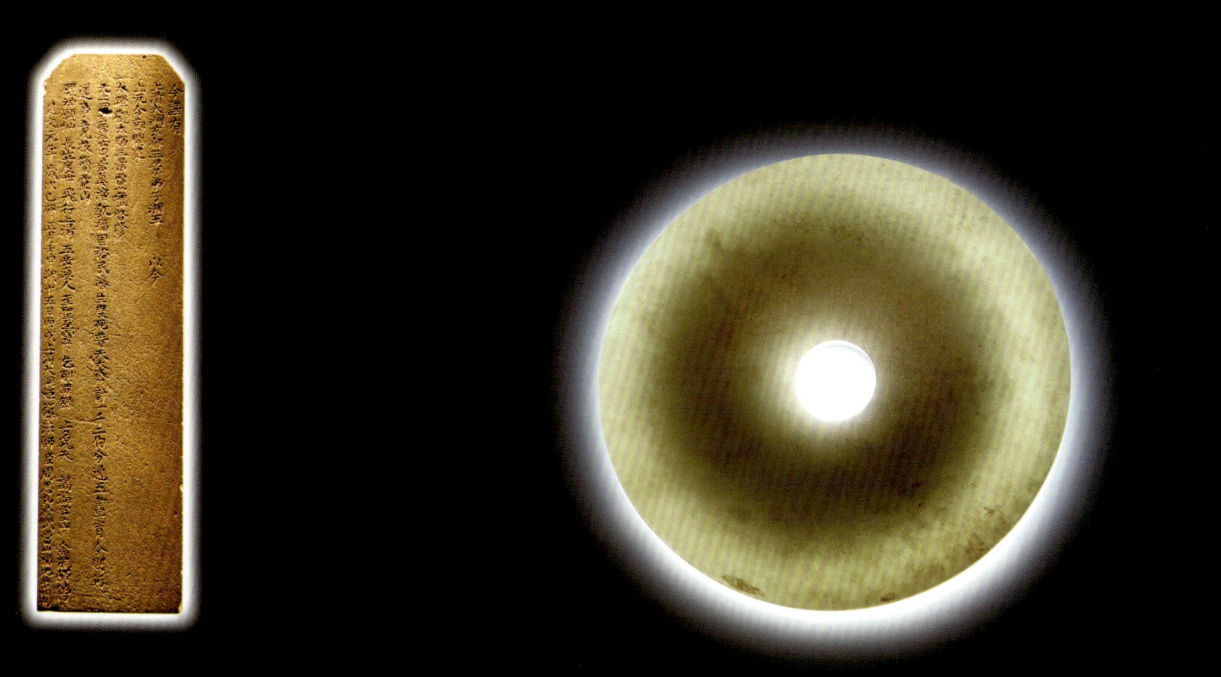

The golden dragon, the round jade with a hole in it, and the bamboo slip used for writing on

The golden dragon, the round jade with a hole in it, and the bamboo slip used for writing on are all unearthed in the Cijian Platform of the Purple Heaven Palace in the Wudang Mountains. The inscription records that during the Lantern Festival in the first year of Jianwen's reign, the Xiangxian King, Zhu Bai (the 12th son's of the Emperor Zhu Yuanzhang) has put in these objects, the golden dragon, the round jade with a hole in it, and the bamboo slip used for writing on, which could communicate with the deity when he established the Luotiandajiao in the Fudi Hall of the Purple Heaven Palace in the Wudang Mountains. The method is to put the jade and the slip onto the golden dragon and then put them into 13 different directions. Since the jade could communicate with the deity, the purpose of this is to send a message of peace to the heaven through these three objects, hoping for the blessing of the Zhenwu God. However, things didn't go smoothly. After several months, under the pressure of the Emperor Jianwen's elimination, he was so afraid of being eliminated, so he committed suicide in his enfeoffment, being a sacrifice of the fight over the imperial power.

The golden dragon is 11.32cm long, 4.5cm wide, and 15gram weight. It is composed two parts as if lift head flying to the heaven. The ripple is clearly to see.

The round jade with a hole in it is 8.06cm diameter and 0.2cm thick with the inner diameter of 1.22cm and 58 gram. In the front is round with a hole in the middle. The whole jade is light green with smooth surface and brightness.

The bamboo slip used for writing on that is also the stele for Taoist rite by Xiang Wang. It is shaped rectangle with slanting shoulder. It is 28.5cm high, 7.2cm wide, 0.7cm thick and 501.5gram weight. The one side has inscripted text and the other side has no text. The text records the things about the whole rite. According to the text, the Xiang Xian King Zhubai set rite in the Purple Heaven Palace on the 15, January of the lunar calendar, 1399, the first year of Emperor Jianwen. The rite is lasting for five days and five nights.

According to the text, there are three ways for putting the bamboo slip. They are mountain, water and earth, choose one of them putting into the fairy mountain, fairy water and fairy land. The mountain slip should match with green round jade, the water one match the gray octagon jade and the earth one match the white square jade. Before put the bamboo slip, people usually use the wood which is 40cm long, 10cm wide and 1cm thick painting in white and gamboges in the frame and red text. The water one uses the cyan paper with red text. The earth one uses yellow paper with red text. When put the slip, usually with one golden dragon, 12 golden Niu and one jade or use 13 golden dragons among which 10 are put in different places and the rest three put with the slip. Different levels of person use different gold, such as the royal family use the pretty one, ordinary use silver to replace gold. Thus we can tell that there must be 12 golden Niu in somewhere in the Purple Heaven Palace, because there is only one golden dragon with the bamboo slip. In ancient times, the dragon has been taken as one of the four intelligence mascots which can bring your wish to the heaven. It is a well wish to the death. In the past, the bamboo slip usually made of wood, but this one is made of green sandstone.

【徐霞客】

徐霞客，名宏祖，号霞客，江苏江阴人。我国古代著名的地理学家，一生博览图经地志，专注于旅行，足迹遍布我国大江南北，他按考察所写的游记，极具地理和文学价值。徐霞客于明天启三年（1623）农历四月游览武当山，写下了《游太和山日记》，记述了在武当山期间的所见所闻，影响颇广。博物馆陈列的徐霞客游览武当山的模拟场景，反映的即是徐霞客游武当山时向道人问道，并得道士馈赠榔梅果，为其母亲回家祝寿的场景。在场景旁边的展柜中，还展示了各种版本的《徐霞客游记》以及其中的《游太和山日记》。

Xu Xiake

Xu Xiake, also named Hongzu or Xiake, is born in the Jiangyin, Jiang Su province. He is the famous geographer and tourist expert in the Ming Dynasty. He read extensively the map and topography, and devoted his mind to tourism. He traveled most of our country and writes many travel notes which has great geographical and literary value. In the April of the lunar calendar in the third year of Tianqi's reign in the Ming Dynasty (the year of 1623), he toured the Wudang Mountains and wrote down *The Diary of Touring the Taihe Mountain* which records what he have seen and heard in the Wudang Mountains with a great influence. This scene displays that when he was learning from the Taoist priest during the Wudang tour, and the Taoist present a gift of langmei fruit to him for his mother's birthday. In the other display cases, you can see his travel notes *Xu Xiake Travel Notes* in different versions and the *The Diary of Touring the Taihe Mountain*.

徐霞客问道武当场景　the scene of Xu Xiake learn from Taoist

游太和山日记

十三日　骑而南趋，石道平敞。三十里，越一石樑，有溪自西东注，即太和下流入汉者。前有碑大书"第一山"三字，乃米襄阳笔，书法飞动，当亦第一。又十里，过草店，襄阳来道，亦至此合。路渐西向，过遇真宫，越雨临下，入坞中。从此西行数里，为趋虚道；南蹄上岭，则走紫霄间道也。登岭。自草店至此，共十里，为回龙观。望嶽顶青紫插天，然相去尚五十里。满山乔木夹道，密佈上下，如行绿慕中。

《游太和山日记》摘要　the abstract of the *Dairy of Travel Taihe Mountain*

太 和 武 当
武当博物馆·道教文化展

仙山名人厅
Mountain with Celebrities Hall

仙山名人厅 072-073
Mountain with Celebrities Hall

仙山名人厅
Mountain with Celebrities Hall

仙山名人厅 Mountain with Celebrities Hall 074-075

治世玄岳·鼎盛尊荣
Zhi Shi Xuan Yue Prosperity Period

道教造像厅
Taoist Josses Hall

武当山无愧于"道教文物宝库"的美誉。现存各类道教造像数千尊,从唐、宋、元、明、清到民国,质地从金、银、铜、铁、锡,到玉、石、砖、木、泥等,其数量之多、等级之高、种类之全、体量之大、工艺水平之高、历史信息之丰富,全国罕见。其中道教造像珍品,多为历代皇室御赐。

Wudang Mountain, known as the treasury of Taoist cultural relics, has preserved thousands of Taoist josses from Tang, Song, Yuan, Ming and Qing Dynasties to the Republic of China with different materials such as gold, sliver, copper, iron, tin, jade, stone, brick, wood, clay etc.. It is rare in the nation for its numerous quantities; high standard level, various type and high technique, abundant historical information among which the Taoist josses are the gem for most of them are granted by the royal families of different dynasties.

真武

真武亦称"玄武",俗称"真武大帝"、"玄天上帝",道教供奉的主神。相传为古静乐国太子,生而神猛,越东海来游,遇天神授以宝剑,入湖北武当山修炼,经四十二年而功成,白日飞升,威镇北方。宋时因避讳改"玄"为"真",称真武。

武当山现存各类不同质地、不同年龄、不同服饰的真武造像近千余尊,大部分为工部在北京铸造好后恭送至武当山供奉。这些造像比例准确、造型生动、形态传神、工艺复杂、制作精细,均为明代皇室敕奉武当山的道教艺术珍品。

Zhen Wu

Zhen Wu, also named Xuan Wu, Emperor Zhen Wu, Emperor Xuan Tian, is the main god that the Taoism sacrificed. In the legend, the prince of Jing Le kingdom is very strong and conferred jade sword by god and cultivated himself in Wudang Mountain, Hubei Province, after 42-year cultivating, he successes to be an immortal mainly in charge of the north part. To avoid the same name with one of the emperor in Song Dynasty, he changed his name Xuan Wu into Zhen Wu.

Now in Wudang Mountain, there are nearly one thousand josses about Zhen Wu in different ages, wearing different clothes with various materials. Most of them are made by the ministry department in Beijing. They are the Taoist treasure which made by the royal families of Ming Dynasty. They have exact proportion, vivid sculpture, lively expression, high technique and fine manufacture.

【玉雕真武坐像】

唐,玉石雕刻,通高92.5cm,重221kg。该造像用一整块玉石雕凿而成,整体呈盘坐修真姿,身着圆领内衣,外罩直领长衫,内袍圆领,外袍开胸,披发跣足,长发披至腰部,盘膝而坐。双手合握,手心向上,左手在下,右手在上置于丹田。面部神情温和祥善,形态为修真内炼状,十分传神。整体雕刻线条简洁、圆润,技法娴熟,是唐代玉雕精品。

jade-carving Zhenwu's sitting statue

The jade-carving Zhenwu's sitting statue, made in Tang Dynasty with the height of 92.5cm and 221kg weight. This statue is made with a whole jade stone shaping the sitting statue of Zhen Wu cultivating himself. He wears a round-neck undergarment and a straight-neck long robe outside. His hair can be clearly seen, and he is sitting tailor-fashion, both hands putting onto the public region, with soft, kind, and smiling facial expression. He forms a posture like practicing, staying still and very vivid. Its carving lines are simple, brief, smooth, and skilled. It is an exquisite jade-carving article of the Tang Dynasty.

【真武太子读书坐像】

明，铜铸鎏金，通高49.5cm，重13.5kg。该太子坐像头梳双髻，面部圆润，表情肃穆，双耳垂大。内穿窄袖贴身内衣，外套广袖右衽长袍，腰系丝绦。双腿盘膝而坐，左掌摊书，右手伸指指看书文。其座呈不规则圆形状，四足外侈。此尊造像是真武幼年在武当山太子坡修道时刻苦学习道经的情形。整尊造像把太子认真钻研道经的神态表现的淋漓尽致。造像背铸阴文共22字，上书"石府王西王村山西平阳府州河十方施主二人等"字样。

prince Zhenwu's reading sitting statue

The prince Zhenwu's reading sitting statue is made in Ming Dynasty. It is copper gilding statue with the height of 49.5cm and 13.5kg. He is round face with solemn expression; ears are very large with hair into two coils. He wears tied undergarment and wide sleeve robe with tie in his waist. He is sitting tailor-fashion, opening the book on his left leg with forefinger of right hand point the text. He is sitting on the irregular round base. This statue reveals the scene of the young Zhenwu's assiduous learning of the Taoist scripture when he was practicing on the Prince Slop in the Wudang Mountains. The whole statue exhibits the vivid expression of prince's carefully researching the Taoist book. In the back of the statue carved the people who give this statue and the place.

【铜铸鎏金戎装真武站像】

明，铜铸鎏金，通高60.2cm，重20.4kg。该站像披发跣足，三目圆睁，身着铠甲，左手前伸掐诀，右手持剑，剑身残佚。两肩飞飘卷起，赤足站立于四足外侈底座上。

copper gild Zhenwu's standing statues in martial attire

The copper gild Zhenwu's standing statues in martial attire is made in Ming Dynasty with the height of 60.2cm and 20.4kg weight. His hair and feet are clearly seen. He opens his eyes, wearing the armour. His left hand is doing thinking while his right hand holds the sword which only the sword handle has preserved with the robe flying. He is standing on the base with no shoes.

【铜铸鎏金真武站像】

明，铜铸鎏金，通高57.5cm，重11.2kg。该站像披发跣足，身着圆领长袍，左手搭于右小臂，右手执剑（剑佚），赤足呈八字形站立于四足方形底座上。

copper gild Zhenwu's standing statues

The copper gild Zhenwu's standing statue made in Ming Dynasty, with 57.5cm high and 11.2kg weight. His hair and feet are clearly seen. He wears a round-neck long robe. His left hand puts on his right arm, right hand hold the sword(the sword lost). He stands on the four-foot square base with his feet apart like the Chinese character "Ba".

【铜铸鎏金戎装真武坐像】

明,铜铸鎏金,通高68.5cm,重44.2kg。该坐像披发跣足,纹理清晰,双耳长厚,脸面圆润,双目微睁,嘴唇紧闭。身穿圆领重铠,佩带护心镜,扎战裙。左右肩头各铸一凸形滚龙。两腿分开,坐在平面神位之上。左手平伸于腹前,大拇指内指,右手握拳,虎口向上,置于大腿腿面。造像整体铸造工艺精湛,形象生动,展现出北方玄天上帝神掌刑罚、诛妖魔的威武形象。

copper gild Zhenwu's sitting statues in martial attire

The copper gild Zhenwu's sitting statues in martial attire made in Ming Dynast with 68.5cm high and 44.2kg weight. The statue's grain is clearly seen. His ears are very large and thick, round face, opening eyes slightly and close mouth. He wears round heavy military attire, mirror which can protect heart and military skirt. There are decorated with dragons on both shoulders. He apart his legs, his left hand before the belly with thumb point inside, right hand makes a fist put on the thigh. The whole statue is made with fine technique and vivid image expressing the mighty figure of Emperor Xuan Tian of north control penalize and kill the demons.

【铜铸鎏金真武坐像】

明，铜铸鎏金，通高75cm，重50.3kg。该坐像披发跣足，内着龙袍，外罩花草边广袖长袍，左手扶膝，右手扶玉带，赤足坐于四卷云足底座上，座右铸一龟蛇。

copper gild Zhenwu's sitting statues

The copper gild Zhenwu's sitting statues is made in Ming Dynasty with the height of 75cm and 50.3kg weight. He wears undergarment and a loose sleeves long robe outside. His left hand put on his knee and right hand hold the jade belt sitting on the base decorated with could. On the right of the base, there is the combination of tortoise and snake.

【铜铸鎏金戎装真武坐像】

明，铜铸鎏金，通高72.5cm，重62.1kg。该坐像披发跣足，面部祥和，身着铠甲，两肩作飞飘，左臂前伸作掐诀，右手仗剑扶于腿部（剑身佚），腰间悬系鲤鱼飘，赤足坐于方形底座，座前两足间铸一龟蛇。通体铜铸鎏金局部彩绘。

copper gild Zhenwu's sitting statues in martial attire

The copper gild Zhenwu's sitting statues in martial attire made in Ming Dynasty with the height of 72.5cm and 62.1kg weight. His hair and feet are clearly seen. His face looks very peaceful. He wears the armour with flying belt. His left hand is doing thinking while his right hand holds the sword put on his leg(only preserved the sword handle). There is belt in his waist. He sits on the square base with the combination of tortoise and snake between his feet. The statue is copper gild with color painting partly.

【铜铸鎏金真武坐像】

明,铜铸鎏金,通高104cm,重83kg。明代民间社团敬奉。此坐像披发跣足,身着广袖长袍,左手置膝,右手扶玉带,赤足间铸一龟蛇。背部作背龛,铸有弥猴献桃、梅鹿衔花、仙鹤、祥云、腾龙、童子、仙人等,足下作四足底座。

copper gild Zhenwu's sitting statues

The copper gild Zhenwu's sitting statues made in Ming Dynasty with the height of 104cm and 83kg weight. It is sacrificed by the voluntary association in the Ming Dynasty. He wears loose sleeve long robe with left hand on the knee and right hand holds the jade belt and the combination of tortoise and snake between his feet. On the back of it, there are the images of a macaque presenting peaches, of a spotted deer holding flowers in the mouth, of an immortal crane, of the auspicious cloud, of the soaring dragon, of boys, of deities, and so on. There is four-foot base underneath.

【铜铸鎏金真武坐像】

明，铜铸鎏金，通高92.5cm，重100.75kg。该像为真武中年坐像，披发跣足，双目微闭，内着圆领龙袍，外罩云龙边广袖蟒袍，左手扶膝，右手握玉带，赤足坐于长方形底座上，两赤足间铸一龟蛇。

copper gild Zhenwu's sitting statues

The copper gild Zhenwu's sitting statues made in Ming Dynasty with the height of 92.5cm and 100.75kg weight. It is a statue of Zhenwu's midlife image, wearing the round-neck undergarment and a loose sleeve robe with his eyes slightly open. His left hand is on his knee and his right hand is on the waistband with jade decoration. He sits on the rectangle base with the combination of tortoise and snake between his feet.

【铜铸鎏金真武坐像】

明，铜铸鎏金，通高54.7cm，重24kg。该造像为真武中年坐像，披发跣足，长须垂至胸前，内着龙袍，外着花草边广袖长袍，左手掐诀置膝，右手扶握玉带，赤足坐于四卷云足底座上，两赤足间铸一龟蛇。

copper gild Zhenwu's sitting statues

The copper gild Zhenwu's sitting statues made in Ming Dynasty with the height of 54.7cm and 24kg weight. It is a statue of Zhenwu's midlife image, wearing the round-neck undergarment and a loose sleeve robe. His left hand is doing thinking and his right hand is on the waistband with jade decoration. He sits on the base with the combination of tortoise and snake between his feet.

【铜铸鎏金真武坐像】

明,铜铸鎏金,该坐像通高77cm,重23.2kg。披发跣足,着直领广袖长袍,左手扶膝,右手握玉带,赤足坐于四足底座上,局部彩绘。

copper gild Zhenwu's sitting statues

The copper gild Zhenwu's sitting statues made in Ming Dynasty with the height of 77cm and 23.2kg weight. He wears straight neck long robe with left hand put on the knee and right hand hold the jade belt, sitting on the base with color painting partly.

【铜铸鎏金真武坐像】

明,铜铸鎏金,通高60.7cm,重28.6kg。该坐像披发跣足,双目微闭,着绣领内衫,外罩花草边广袖龙袍,左手仰伸掐诀,右手垂扶于膝,赤足坐于平底底座上,两足间铸一龟蛇。

copper gild Zhenwu's sitting statues

The copper gild Zhenwu's sitting statues made in Ming Dynasty with the height of 60.7cm and 28.6kg weight. He closes his eyes slightly and wears undergarment and loose sleeve outside. His left hand is doing thinking while his right hand put on his knee with the combination of tortoise and snake between his feet.

【铜铸鎏金真武坐像】

明，铜铸鎏金，通高98.3cm，重59kg。该坐像披发跣足（头顶局部下凹），内着圆领龙袍，外罩广袖长袍，左手掐诀，右手扶膝，赤足坐于四足底座上，两足间底座凹陷处铸一龟蛇。

copper gild Zhenwu's sitting statues

The copper gild Zhenwu's sitting statues made in Ming Dynasty with the height of 98.3cm and 59kg weight. The top of the head is sinking partly. He wears the round-neck undergarment and a loose sleeve robe. His left hand is doing thinking while his right hand put on his knee. He sits on the four-foot base with the combination of tortoise and snake between his feet.

【铜铸鎏金真武坐像】

明，铜铸鎏金，通高86cm，重43.2kg。该坐像披发跣足，面带微笑，目视前方。身着圆领长袍，左手扶膝，右手握腰带，赤足坐于四卷云足底座上，造型生动、自然。

copper gild Zhenwu's sitting statues

The copper gild Zhenwu's sitting statues made in Ming Dynasty with the total height of 86cm and 43.2kg weight, smiling and looking forward. He wears the round-neck long robe with his left hand on his knee and his right hand is on the waistband with jade decoration. He sits on the rectangle base. The statue is vivid and lifelike.

道教造像厅 090-091
Taoist Josses Hall

【太乙救苦天尊】

明，铜铸鎏金，通高106.7cm，重53.2kg。此造像头戴莲花冠，身披道袍，衣纹舒展，和蔼可亲，面容慈祥。左手扶凭几，右手仰指，双腿盘坐于莲花座上，座下为其坐骑青狮。太乙救苦天尊为统领（青玄左府）一切真仙之神，掌握着三界（人、鬼、神）救苦之事。为了普度众生，他有很多的化身，最著名的是化为"十方救苦天尊"。传说他身穿九色云霞羽服，乘狮子玉莲宝座，左手执甘露玉净瓶，右手执青枝。

The taiyi salvation god

This statue made in Ming Dynasty, copper gilding with the height of 106.7cm and 53.2kg. He wears lotus-like head. His left hand holds the belt and right hand lift up, sitting on the lotus like pedestal holding by the lion. The clothes lines of it are smooth and stretching. It is kind and amiable. The Taiyi Salvation God is the deity who rules all other real deities (where called the Qing Xuan Zuo Fu), taking the salvation affairs of the three worlds (human, ghost, and deity) in his control. For the purpose of saving all living creatures, he has got many an embodiment, among which "the Shifang Salvation God" is the most famous one. It is said that he wears a nine-color-cloud feather clothes, riding on a lion over the jade lotus pedestal, with his left hand holding an amrita jade vase and his right hand holding a cyan branch.

九曜星君

星宿名，道教尊崇的星神。九尊站像均为铜铸鎏金质地，局部彩绘，其冠饰、盔甲、姿态、神情各异，造型生动，铸造工艺精良，是明皇室御赐武当山宫观的塑像精品。

道经云：天有九曜，即日曜、月曜、火曜、水曜、木曜、金曜、土曜、罗候、计都九星。此九星因照耀世间，故名九曜。九曜九年循环，古人多以人命吉凶视之，认为会影响人生祸福。据《北斗本生经》记载：古代有一周御王，圣德无边，其爱妃紫光夫人，明哲慈惠，夫人发下大愿，要为国王生下圣子，辅佐乾坤。一年春天，夫人在金莲花温玉池洗澡，忽有所感，生莲花九苞，化生九子。两长子一为天皇大帝，一为紫微大帝，七幼子为北斗七星。该王妃即为道教所供奉的斗姆神。

nine-yao xingjun

The nine-yao xingjun is the name of the constellation, worshiped by Taoism. These nine xingjun have diversified shapes, facial expressions, clothes, and postures, vivid and lifelike. They are all copper gilded, being the exquisite articles founded under the bestowal of the royalty in the Ming Dynasty in the palaces and temples in the Wudang Mountains.

In the Taoist books, there are nine yao in heaven, the sun yao, the moon yao, the fire yao, the water yao, the wood yao, the gold yao, the earth yao, luohou, and jidu. These nine stars shines all over the earth, so they are called nine yao. The nine yao have a nine-year circulation, as indication of people's good and ill luck in the ancient time, influencing people's life. According to *The Big Dipper Bensheng Sculpture*, in the ancient time, there was a Yu Emperor in the Zhou Dynasty, being saint boundlessly. He had a wise and kind concubine who he loved so much, called Madam Ziguang. She prayed hardly to bear sons for the king in order to help him handle the state affairs. One spring, when she was bathing in the golden lotus wenyu pool, she felt something and gave birth to nine lotus buds which became nine sons. Of the two elders of them, one is the Great Tianhuang Emperor, and the other is the Great Ziwei Emperor. Other younger sons are the big dipper. This concubine is the Doumu Deity worshiped by Taoism.

【铜铸鎏金北斗九曜星君站像】

明，铜铸鎏金，通高57.9cm，重23.1kg。该站像头戴翼善冠，面部表情肃穆，颈系披肩，左臂前伸持法器，右臂扬伸呈握拳状，脚踏战靴呈八字形，局部彩绘。

copper gilding big-dipper nine-yao xingjun's standing statues

The copper gilding big-dipper nine-yao xingjun's standing statue is made in Ming Dynasty, copper gilding with color painting partly, 57.9cm high and 23.1kg weight. This statue had Yishan hat with solemn facial expression. He wears cappa. His left arm stretch forward to hold Taoist instrument and right arm form a fist. He wears battle boots standing apart both feet.

明，铜铸鎏金，通高57cm，重20.2kg。该站像头戴翼善冠，头与身体左倾，身着铠甲，外披战袍，双手执械至腰间，双足着战靴呈八字形站立，通体彩绘饰金。

This statue is made in Ming Dynasty, copper gilding with color painting, 57cm high and 20.2kg weight. This statue had Yishan hat and incline to the left with his body. He wears armour and coat armour outside. His hands hold weapon, wearing battle boots standing apart both feet.

明，铜铸鎏金，通高58.9cm，重18.1kg。该站像头戴法箍，披发，身着铠甲，胸前戴护心镜，两肩作飞飘，左肩前伸（左手残佚），右臂扬伸执法器，脚踏战靴呈八字形站立，通体彩绘饰金。

This is made in Ming Dynasty, copper gilding with color painting, 58.9cm high and 18.1kg weight. This statue had Fa hat with hair scattered. He wears armour with protection mirror in his chest. There are flutter belt on his shoulder. He stretch forward his left shoulder (hand lost) and right arm lift holding Taoist instrument. He wears battle boots standing apart both feet.

道教造像厅 094-095
Taoist Josses Hall

明，铜铸鎏金，通高62.9cm，重23.1kg。该站像头戴武冠，三目圆睁，颈部系有披肩，内着铠甲，外罩战袍，双手捧一桃形器，桃内作一人物，脚踏战靴呈八字形站立，通体彩绘饰金。

This is made in Ming Dynasty, copper gilding with color painting, 62.9cm high and 23.1kg weight. This statue had Wu hat with three eyes widely open. He wears cappa, armour and coat armor outside. He holds a kind of instrument. He wears battle boots standing apart both feet.

明，铜铸鎏金，通高60.8cm，重21.9kg。该站像头戴法箍，身着铠甲，左臂略屈伸，右臂曲张握械（械佚），脚踏战靴呈八字形站立，通体彩绘饰金。

This is made in Ming Dynasty, copper gilding with color painting, 60.8cm high and 21.9kg weight. This statue had Fa hat. He wears armour with left arm slightly bent forward and right arm hold weapon (weapon lost). He wears battle boots standing apart both feet.

明，铜铸鎏金，通高62.5cm，重21.4kg。该站像头戴武冠，怒目圆睁，面部狰狞，身着铠甲，左手持械，右手仰伸，身形左倾，脚穿战靴呈八字形站立，通体彩绘饰金。

This statue is made in Ming Dynasty, copper gilding with color painting, 62.5cm high and 21.4kg weight. This statue had Wu hat with solemn facial expression. He wears armour. His hands hold weapon, wearing battle boots standing apart both feet.

明，铜铸鎏金，通高59.5cm，重22.9kg。该站像头戴武冠，内着铠甲，外罩战袍，双手合握，脚踏战靴呈八字形站立，通体铜铸彩绘饰金。

This statue is made in Ming Dynasty, copper gilding with color painting, 59.5cm high and 22.9kg weight. This statue had Wu hat. He wears armour and coat armour outside. His hands holds together, wearing battle boots standing apart both feet.

明，铜铸鎏金，通高57.3cm，重21.7kg。该站像头戴武冠，身着铠甲，身体右倾，左臂曲伸，右臂前伸（右手指残），脚穿战靴呈八字形站立，通体彩绘饰金。

This is made in Ming Dynasty, copper gilding with color painting, 57.3cm high and 21.7kg weight. This statue had Wu hat wearing armour with body inclined to the right side. He bent his left arm and stretch forward right arm (lost finger). He wears battle boots standing apart both feet.

明，铜铸鎏金，通高55.2cm，重19kg。该站像头戴法箍，披发，内着铠甲，外罩战袍，左臂曲伸捻指，右臂前曲持法器，赤足呈八字形站立，通体彩绘饰金。

This is made in Ming Dynasty, copper gilding with color painting, 55.2cm high and 19kg weight. This statue had Fa hat with hair scattered. He wears armour and coat armor outside. He bent his left arm and stretch forward right arm holding Taoist instrument. He wears battle boots standing apart both feet.

【斗姆坐像】

明，铜铸鎏金，通高61.4cm，重17.9kg。斗姆为道教尊奉的星斗神系主神，心地慈爱，深受民间崇奉。人们无论贫富贵贱，只要诚心礼拜，口念斗姆名号，就能消灾辟邪，延年益寿。其造型为六臂，面部慈祥，和蔼可亲，其中两手执日月法器、两手合掌、两手掐诀掌握镜棒，盘坐于卷云足莲花座上，底座上铸有一只麒麟和四尊力士像，将斗姆高高托起，造型生动，惟妙惟肖。

Doumu's sitting statue

This is made in Ming Dynasty, copper gilding, 61.4cm high and 17.9kg weight. Doumu is the main deity of the star deity system worshiped by Taoism. Doumu is so kind-hearted that no matter the person is poor or rich, as long as he worships in earnest and read the name of Doumu, any disaster or misfortune will disappear, and his life will be prolonged. This statue has six arms, hunkering on the lotus pedestal, with its both hands holding the sun-and-moon instrument, hands closed, and clutching the jue and holding the stick. Her facial expression has a kind and amiable feature. The pedestal has a kylin and four statues of Lishi which uphold Doumu. The whole statue is vivid.

【水母】

(左)明，铜铸鎏金，通高64.5cm，重15.2kg。
(右)明，铜铸鎏金，通高63.6cm，重20.8kg。

道教民间水神。传说由太上老君指派，专管天下水情，百姓称之为水母娘娘。凡遇河水断流，天下大旱，百姓皆向其祈祷施雨，水母娘娘遂将随身携带的圣瓶向下洒之，天下便普降甘露，旱情解除。这两尊水母坐像，均头戴凤冠，面部表情凝重，一手扶膝，一手掐诀，赤足坐于龙托莲花座上，人物塑造细腻、传神。

The water mother

These two statues are made in Ming Dynasty, copper gilding with colour painting, the right one is 63.6cm high and 20.8kg weight, the other is 64.5cm high and 15.2kg weight.

She is the folk water deity in Taoism. It is said that she is assigned by Tai Shang Lao Jun to manage the water condition, so the public call her the water mother empress. Once the river suffers the water break and there is a drought, the public will all pray towards her for rain, and then the water mother empress will reverse the sacred vase which she carries with her and sprinkle downward. At that time, the rain will come and resolve the drought. These two water mother statues in this showcase have a worried facial expression, seeming to concern about the public. One hand put on the knee and the other hand do thinking. The characters are carved so exquisitely and accurately, sitting on the lotus pedestal held up by a dragon.

关天君

亦称关帝，东汉末年蜀将，姓关名羽，字云长。东汉献帝授以汉寿亭侯，自汉以降，历代封建统治者均将其视作"忠义"的化身，名位越来越高，由侯而王，旋而晋帝。在唐代，关羽被列为古今六十名将之一；宋代被冠以"武圣"；宋徽宗时封"义勇武安王"；元文宗时封"壮缪义勇武安显灵英济王"；明神宗时封"三界伏魔大帝神威远震天尊关圣帝君"，把关羽庙称为武庙，与孔子文庙并列。武当山关帝庙即是明万历皇帝为其封帝后专建之庙堂。道教乃多神崇拜，关羽在道教中又被尊奉为真武护法，位居六大帅之列，在民间还被尊崇为武财神。

Guantianjun

Guantianjun is also called the Guan emperor, a general of the Kingdom of Shu in the late Eastern Han Dynasty. His family name is Guan, his first name is Yu, and he named himself Yunchang. The Xian Emperor in the Eastern Han Dynasty names him Han Shou Ting Hou, and all the feudal rulers since the Han Dynasty consider him as the embodiment of "fidelity", with his status moving higher and higher, from Hou to King, and then to the emperor. In the Tang Dynasty, Guan Yu was listed as one of the 60 famous generals throughout the history; in the Song Dynasty, he was called "the military king"; during the reign of the Song Huizong, he was named "the brave Wu'an King"; during the reign of the Yuan Wenzong, he was named "the strong and brave wu'an king"; during the reign of the Ming Shenzong, he was named "the great three-world evil-destroying king Guanshengdijun". The Temple of Guanyu is called the Military Temple, in parallel with the temple of Confucius. The Guan Emperor Temple in the Wudang Mountains is just the one specially built under the command of the Ming Wanli Emperor after Guan's naming of emperor. Taoism is a kind of religion worshiping multiple deities, and Guanyu is honored to be one of the protectors of the Zhenwu God, listed in the six great generals. Guanyu is also respected and named the military god of wealth by the folk people.

【铜铸关天君站像】

明，铜铸鎏金，通高56cm，重15.5kg。该站像通体彩绘，头扎巾纶，身着战袍，脚蹬战靴。右手做倒提长刀状（长刀佚），昂首挺胸站立于椭圆形瑞云纹底座上。

copper Guan Tianjun standing statue

This statue is made in Ming Dynasty, copper gilding with color painting, 56cm high and 15.5kg weight. This statue had Jin hat and wears armour and battle boots. His right hand hold weapon standing on the oval pedestal decorated with auspicious cloud.

道教造像厅
Taoist Josses Hall

明，铜质，通高66.6cm，重14.5kg。该站像通体彩绘，局部饰金，头扎巾纶，身披铠甲，脚蹬战靴，左手捻须，右手执长刀（长刀佚），站立于束腰四足底座上。

This statue is made in Ming Dynasty, copper with color painting partly gold, 66.6cm high and 14.5kg weight. This statue had Jin hat and wears armour and battle boots. His left hand holds his beard and right hand hold weapon standing on the four-foot pedestal.

明，铜铸彩绘，通高62.1cm，重9.1kg。该站像通体彩绘，头戴雷巾，丹眉凤目，左手做捻须状，右手执长刀（刀佚），内着铠甲，外罩战袍，脚踏战靴，呈八字形站立于底座上（右脚、底座残佚）。

This statue is made in Ming Dynasty, copper with colour painting, 62.1cm high and 9.1kg weight. He wears kerchief and thick eyebrow and big eyes. He hold long sword (the sword lost) on the right hand and entwist his beard with his left hand. He wears armour inside with coat armor outside. He wears caliga standing on the square base (the right foot and the base are lost).

明，铜铸，通高55.3cm，重18.6kg。该站像头戴雷巾，丹眉凤目，长髯飘飘，左手插腰，右手执刀（刀佚），脚踏战靴呈八字形站立于束腰四外撇足方形底座上。

This standing statue is made in Ming Dynasty, copper, 55.3cm high and 18.6kg weight, wearing kerchief and thick eyebrow and big eyes. He has long beard and put his left hand on his waist with sword(sword lost) on the right hand. He wears caliga standing on the square base.

明，铜铸，通高56.6cm，重10.9kg。该站像通体饰金，局部彩绘。头戴雷巾，丹眉凤目，内着铠甲，外罩战袍，左手插腰，右臂前屈握长刀（刀佚），脚踏战靴呈八字形站立于四细高足方形底座上。

Made in Ming Dynasty, copper, 56.6cm high and 10.9kg weight. This standing statue decorated with gold, partly colour painting. He wears kerchief and thick eyebrow and big eyes. He has long coat armor and put his left hand on his waist with long sword on the right hand(the sword lost). He wears caliga standing on the square base.

明，铜铸，通高52.5cm，重8.7kg。该站像头戴雷巾，丹眉凤目，左手捻长须，右臂前屈握长刀（刀佚），身着铠甲，脚踏战靴，呈八字形站立于束腰方形四外撇足底座上。

Made in Ming Dynasty, copper, 52.5cm high and 8.7kg weight. This standing statue wears kerchief and thick eyebrow and big eyes. He hold long sword(sword lost) on the right hand and entwist his beard with his left hand. He wears armour and caliga standing on the square base.

道教造像厅
Taoist Josses Hall

明，铜铸鎏金，通高58.2cm，重8.9kg。该站像丹眉凤目，通体饰金，头戴幞头巾，左手扬执长刀，右手捻长须，内着铠甲，外罩战袍，两肩作长飘带（带局部残），脚踏战靴，呈八字形站立于四足方形底座上。

This standing statue is made in Ming Dynasty, copper gild, 58.2cm high and 8.9kg weight, decorated with gold. He wears kerchief and thick eyebrow and big eyes. He hold long sword on the left hand and entwist his beard with his right hand. He wears armour inside with coat armor outside. The flying ribbon on his shoulder (the ribbon lost partly). He wears caliga standing on the square base.

【圣公坐像】

明，铜铸鎏金，通高103.4cm，重53.8kg。该坐像头戴王冠，身着广袖长袍，双手握笏板，着卷云履坐于卷云底座上。圣公、圣母为真武的父母，原为静乐国国王和皇后，在武当山各宫观父母殿均有供奉。

saint father sitting statue

This statue is made in Ming Dynasty, copper gilding, 103.4cm high and 53.8kg weight. This statue had crown and wears loose sleeve long robe. His hands hold Wuban, sitting on the Juan Yun pedestal. The saint father and the saint mother are the parents of Zhenwu, originally the king and the queen of the Jingle Kingdom. There is a special place, the Parents Hall, for offering in the Wudang Mountains.

道教造像厅 104–105
Taoist Josses Hall

【圣母坐像】

明，铁铸，通高59.6cm，重8.1kg。该坐像头戴凤冠，挽高髻，身着广袖长袍，双手捧握朝板，腰悬如意花结，脚穿云履坐于四足底座上，局部座残。

saint mother sitting statue

This statue is made in Ming Dynasty, iron, 59.6cm high and 8.1kg weight. This statue had phoenix crown and her hair fixed on the head. She wears loose sleeve long robe with Chaoban in her hands and decorated with Ruyi in her waist sitting on the four-foot pedestal which has partly lost.

【铜铸道童站像】

明，铜铸，通高81.1cm，重37.1kg。该造像头部挽髻，外披卷草边道装，双手捧一药葫芦，脚穿云履，站立于四卷云纹底座上。

copper Taoist child standing statue

This statue is made in Ming Dynasty, copper, 81.1cm high and 37.1kg weight. This statue had his hair fix on the head and wears Taoist clothes holding a gourd-like medicine bottle. He stands on the pedestal decorated with auspicious clound.

【铜铸金童站像】

明，铜铸鎏金，通高100.8cm，重30.6kg，为真武侍神。该站像头戴翼善冠，身着云纹广袖长袍，双手拱捧，隐于袖间，其表情凝重，体态修长，腰间悬系如意花结，足穿云履。

The copper golden boy standing statue

This statue is made in Ming Dynasty, copper gilding, 100.8cm high and 30.6kg weight. He is the serving deity of Zhenwu, wearing a yishan hat and a pair of cloud shoes, with dignified expression, both hands folding and hiding under the sleeves. He has wide sleeves and long robe. He is strong and tall, the ruyi knot hanging from his waist.

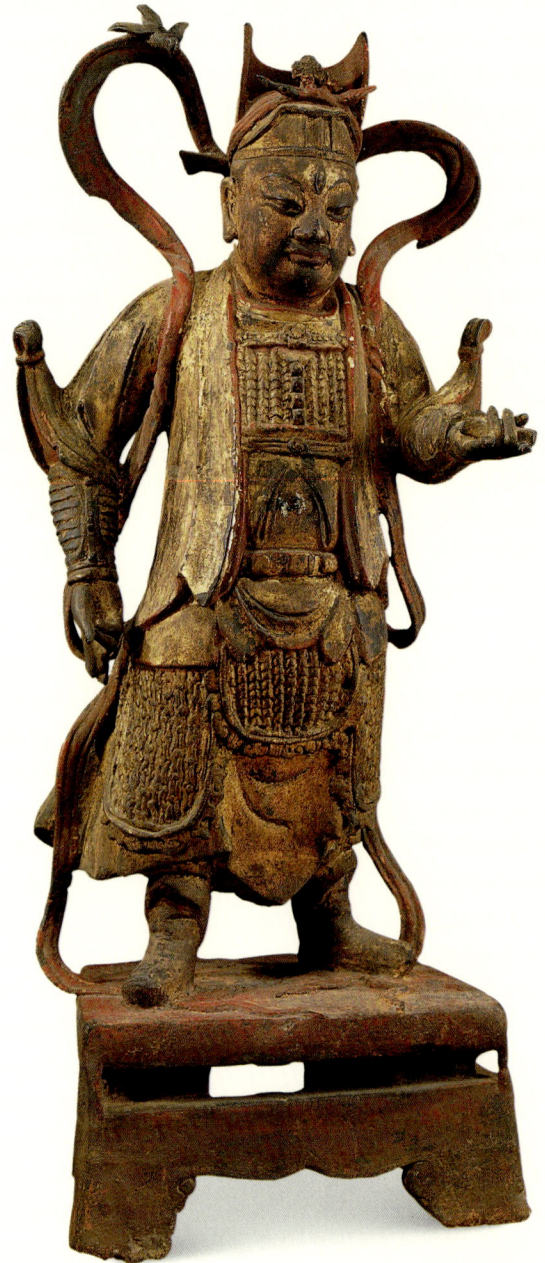

【乌鸦神】

明，铜铸鎏金，通高62.7cm，重17.2kg。该站像整体保存完整，头戴翼善冠，身披铠甲，肩部飘带飞起，飘带顶部铸一乌鸦，左手握一长方形法器，右手作剑指，脚踏战靴站立于四卷云足方形底座上。

The crow deity

This statue is made in Ming Dynasty, copper gilding, 62.7cm high and 17.2kg weight. The whole statue preserved well. He wears Yishan hat and armour, a crown standing on the top of his flutter belt. His left hand holds a rectangle Taoist instrument and right hand shaping the sword finger. He wears battle boots standing on the square pedestal decorated with auspicious cloud.

传说真武太子初入武当时，有乌鸦引路，黑虎巡山。修炼时，有乌鸦报晓，黑虎护山。太子在得道成仙后，封黑虎为巡山黑虎大元帅，封乌鸦为乌鸦神。武当山在乌鸦岭还专门敕建有乌鸦庙，并塑乌鸦神像奉祀。每年香客信士到武当山进香时均要带玉米、小麦等谷物抛洒空中，喂食乌鸦。乌鸦接食时，场面壮观，历史上将其称为"乌鸦接食"，为武当山"动八景"中著名的一景。

It is said that when the prince Zhenwu first entered Wudang, he has the crow for his road guider and the black tiger for his mountain patrolman; when he practicing, the crow reports time for him and the black tiger protects the mountain. After the prince becoming the god and the emperor, he named the black tiger to be the marshal and the crow to be the deity. Originally there was a crow temple in the crow mountain and a crow statue for sacrificing. Every year, believers will come to Wudang to pray, taking corn, wheat, and others with them to feed crows. The scene of the crow's receiving food is very spectacular, which is one of the eight famous dynamic landscapes in the Wudang Mountains, called "the crow's receiving food" in history.

道教造像厅 108–109
Taoist Josses Hall

【龙神】

明，铜铸鎏金，通高63.5cm，重13.7kg。该龙神为鱼面人形象，身着铠甲，左手屈伸，右手置腰部持械（械佚），腰悬鲤鱼飘，脚踏战靴战立于方形卷云足底座上。

The dragon deity

This statue is made in Ming Dynasty, copper gild, 63.5cm high and 13.7kg weight. He has the fish face and human body wearing armour. His left hand bent and right hand holds weapon(the weapon lost). There are Liyu belt on his waist and standing on the square pedestal decorated with auspicious cloud.

龙神为传说中统领水族的王，掌管兴云降雨。龙神按方位分为"五帝龙王"，以海洋又分为"四海龙王"。唐玄宗时，诏祠龙池，设坛官致祭，以祭雨师之仪祭龙王。宋太祖沿用唐代祭五龙之制，宋徽宗大观二年（1108）诏天下五龙皆封王爵。封青龙神为广仁王，赤龙神为嘉泽王，黄龙神为孚应王，白龙神为义济王，黑龙神为灵泽王。该两尊龙神一尊为南方火龙神，即赤龙神嘉泽王；另一尊为北方黑龙神灵泽王。

【龙神】

明，铜铸鎏金，通高67.1cm，重10.9kg。该站像为龙面人身，着长袍，双手捧握笏板，笏板上铸有"火龙神"三字，腰垂鲤鱼飘，脚穿云履站立于四卷云足方形底座上，座残。

The dragon deity

He is made in Ming Dynasty, copper gild, 67.1cm high and 10.9kg weight. He has the dragon face and human body wearing long robe with Wuban on his hands. There is the Chinese character which means fire dragon god on the Wuban. There are Liyu belt on his waist and standing on the square pedestal decorated with auspicious cloud.

According to the legend, the dragon deity is the king of the aquatic animals, and it can control the cloud and rain. The dragon deity can be divided into "five dragon kings", and according to the sea, it can also be divided into "four sea dragon kings". During the reign of Emperor Xuanzong of Tang Dynasty, in the Cilong Pool, he established an altar to worship the dragon king in the way of worshiping the rain god. The Emperor Taizu of Song Dynasty has followed the system of worshiping the five dragons of the Tang Dynasty. In the second year of the Song Huizong's reign (the year 1108), Song Huizong named all the five dragons in the rank of nobility, the cyan dragon deity as the Guangren emperor, the red dragon deity as the Jiaze Emperor, the yellow dragon deity as the Fuying emperor, the white dragon deity as the Yiji emperor, and the black dragon deity as the Lingze emperor. Of these two dragon deities displayed in this showcase, one is the South fire dragon deity, i.e. the red dragon deity, the Jiaze emperor, and the other is the North black dragon deity, the Lingze emperor.

【九天玄女】

　　九天玄女，亦称玄女、九天娘娘，原是中国古代神话中的女神，后为道教所信仰，成为神系中仅次于西王母的女神，黄帝之师。《皇帝内传》记："帝与蚩尤战不胜，玄女为帝制夔牛鼓八十面，遂破蚩尤。"这实际上是以原始社会氏族部落之兼并战争与神仙结合为一体的传说故事，是祖先崇拜与神仙崇拜的神化在道教里的反映。这组九天娘娘与侍奉仙女造像是武当山遗存的一组铜铸宋代造像，神像造型修长、典雅，项饰、衣饰、面部雕刻等方面均属宋代的雕刻风格，是武当山现存文物中的宋代铜铸造像精品。

The Goddess of the Empyrean

　　The Goddess of the Empyrean is also called the Goddess or the Empyrean Empress. It was originally the deity in the Chinese ancient legend, and later it is worshiped by Taoism, becoming the goddess just ranking after the fairy God-Mother in the deity system and the teacher of the Emperor Huang. In *The Biography of the Emperor*, it said that "the Emperor could not defeat Chiyou, and then the Goddess made him eighty kuiniu drums, so he defeated Chiyou". Actually this is a legendary story combining the annexation fight between the tribes in the primitive society with the deity, and it is the reflection of the deification of the worship of the ancestor and the deity in Taoism. This set of the Empyrean Empress and handmaid statues is a group of statues of the Song Dynasty remaining in the Wudang Mountains, with slender shape, and the necklace, the clothes decoration, and the form of the visage all have some features of the Song Dynasty. It is an exquisite copper article of the Song Dynasty remaining in the Wudang Mountains.

道教造像厅
Taoist Josses Hall

    1. 宋，铜铸鎏金，通高70.1cm，重11.9kg。该站像头戴凤冠，着花草边广袖长袍，左臂前曲伸，掌心向上，右臂略扬，脚穿云履站立于四卷云足底座上，整体铜铸鎏金。

    2. 宋，铜铸鎏金，通高73.1cm，重13.9kg。该站像着凤冠，面部祥和，身穿卷草边广袖长袍，双手合捧一铜花，踏云履站立于四卷云足底座，整体铜铸。

    3. 宋，铜铸鎏金，通高72.7cm，重13.6kg。该站像头戴凤冠，身着花草边广袖长袍，双手合捧印，着云履，站立于四卷云足底座，整体铜铸。

    Ⅰ. The left statue is made in Song Dynasty, copper gilding, 70.1cm high and 11.9kg weight. This statue had Phoenix hat and wears loose sleeve long robe. Her left arm bent with palm upward and right arm slightly lift up. She is standing on the pedestal decorated with auspicious cloud.

    Ⅱ. The middle statue is made in Song Dynasty, copper gilding, 73.1cm high and 13.9kg weight. This statue had Phoenix hat with peaceful facial expression. She wears loose sleeve long robe holding the copper flower standing on the pedestal decorated with auspicious cloud.

    Ⅲ. The right statue is made in Song Dynasty, copper gilding, 72.7cm high and 13.6kg weight. This statue had Phoenix hat and wears loose sleeve long robe. She holds the seal standing on the pedestal decorated with auspicious cloud.

【执旗、捧剑】

执旗、捧剑又名水、火二将，与周公、桃花均为真武祖师侍神。这两尊造像，刻画细腻，性格鲜明，铸造工艺精湛。

Zhiqi and Pengjian

Zhiqi and Pengjian are also called the generals of water and fire, being the serving deities of the Zhenwu God together with Zhougong and Taohua. These two statues are of exquisite carving technique, of sharp-cut character, and of consummate founding craftsmanship.

执旗，明，铜铸鎏金，通高67.1cm，重25.3kg。该站像头戴武冠，身着铠甲，肩部飘带飞起，两手前屈，合执旌旗（旗佚），脚踏战靴，站立于四马蹄足方形底座上。

Zhiqi, made in Ming Dynasty, copper gild, 67.1cm high and 25.3kg weight. This statue wears Wu hat and armour with flying ribbon on the shoulder. His hands bent before chest just like holding the flag(the flag lost). He wears caliga standing on the horseshoe base.

道教造像厅
Taoist Josses Hall 114 –115

捧剑，明，铜铸鎏金，通高66.5cm，重23.6kg。该站像头戴武冠，净面无须，双肩飘带飞扬，双手合捧宝剑（剑佚），身着铠甲，脚踏战靴，站立于四马蹄足方形底座上。

Pengjian, made in Ming Dynasty, copper gild, 66.5cm high and 23.6kg weight. This staue wears Wu hat with no beard and flying ribbon on the shoulder. He holds sword(the sword lost) wearing armour and caliga standing on the horeshoe base.

【铜铸鎏金侍女站像】

两侍女站像均身着花草边广袖长袍，双手合捧花朵形供器，头顶作双髻，脚穿云履站立于四卷云足底座。侍女在道教神系中常与金童、执旗、捧剑一同侍立于真武祖师座前两侧，她们在神仙神系中级别虽然不高，但位置较为重要。

copper gild maid standing statue

The two maid standing statues are wearing loose sleeve long robe and hold the sacrifice instrument shaping like flower. Their hair fix on the head as two knot standing on the pedestal decorated with auspicious cloud. In Taoism, the maid usually stands beside the Zhenwu God together with golden boy, zhiqi, and pengjian. Although they are not in a high status of the deity system, they occupy a comparatively important position.

宋，铜铸鎏金，通高71.7cm，重17.1kg。该站像挽发，结双髻，内着裙衫，外罩广袖长袍，双手合捧一碟，内置莲花型物一。脚穿卷云履，站立于卷云底座上。

This statue is made in Song Dynasty, copper gild, 71.7cm high and 17.1kg weight, having her hair worn in two coils and wearing skirt robe inside with loose sleeve, long robe outside. Her hands hold a plate with lotiform things in it. She stands on the base.

宋，铜铸鎏金，通高72.1cm，重15.8kg。该站像头挽双髻，内着裙衫，外罩广袖长袍，双手合捧一碟，内置莲花型物一。脚穿卷云履，站立于卷云底座上。

It made in Song Dynasty, copper gild, 72.1cm high and 15.8kg weight. This statue has her hair worn in two coils, wearing skirt robe inside with loose sleeve, long robe outside. Her hands hold a plate with lotiform things in it standing on the base.

道教造像厅 116–117
Taoist Josses Hall

【捧印侍女站像】
maid holding seal standing statue

明，铜铸鎏金，通高74.3cm，重16.8kg。该站像挽发，通体彩绘，内着裙衫，外罩广袖长袍，双手捧印，腰间垂悬如意花结，着云头履，站立于外侈方形底座上。

This statue is made in Ming Dynasty, copper gild, 74.3cm high and 16.8kg weight, colour painting and has her hair worn in coil and wearing loose sleeve, long robe and Ruyi on her waist. Her hands hold seal standing on the square base.

明，铜铸鎏金，通高67.5cm，重14.2kg。该站像挽发，局部彩绘，着卷云广袖长衫，双手捧印，着云头履，站立于四卷云外侈方形底座上。

This statue is made in Ming Dynasty, copper gild, 67.5cm high and 14.2kg weight, partly colour painting and has her hair worn in coil and wearing loose sleeve, long robe. Her hands hold seal standing on the square base.

【五显灵官】

五显灵官是道教五百灵官的五位统帅，也称大圣华光五大灵官。灵官在道教神像中有几种：一是天府中的小神与仙曹并称，另有十天灵官、九地灵官、水府灵官；二是五百灵官；三是五显灵官；四是王灵官。此五尊造像均为铜铸鎏金质地，局部使用彩绘。其造型迥异，别具一格。冠带、衣甲、容貌、塑造各具特色，人物形象带有鲜明的西域文化特征。

The five Xianling officials

They are five commanders in chief of the 500 Ling officials, also called the five great Huaguang Ling officials. There are several sorts of Ling officials in the Taoist statues. The first one is the combination of the godling and the deity, as well as ten heaven Ling officials, nine earth Ling officials, and the water Ling official. The second one is the 500 Ling officials. The third one is the five Xianling officials, and the fourth one is the Wangling official. These five statues are all copper gild with color painting partly with different sculpt. Their clothes, facial expression have unique features with bright cultural characteristic of the western region.

1. 明，铜铸鎏金，局部彩绘，通高64.2cm，重18.6kg。该站像头戴小盔，红发红须，身着铠甲，外系短袍，双手呈左下右上姿，合持一器（器佚），脚踏战靴，站立于四足底座上。

2. 明，铜铸鎏金，局部彩绘，通高65.5cm，重17.4kg。该站像头戴筒帽，两鬓发角上抒，面部须发张扬，身着铠甲，外系短袍，左手屈伸握拳至腰际，右臂略屈执鞭形械（械佚），脚踏战靴，呈八字形站立于四足底座上。

3. 明，铜铸鎏金，局部彩绘，通高64.4cm，重22.9kg。该站像束发戴法箍，怒目圆睁，身着铠甲，双手合捧虎头印，脚踏战靴，呈八字形站立于四足底座上。

4. 明，铜铸鎏金，局部彩绘，通高66.1cm，重23.3kg。该站像头戴幞头冠，身着圆领广袖长袍，双手合执经卷，立于四足底座上。

5. 明，铜铸鎏金，局部彩绘，通高63.1cm，重21.2kg。该站像头戴三梁小盔，两鬓发须飞扬，身着铠甲，外罩短袍，左手执钉榫形法器，右手曲伸执器（器佚）呈击打状，脚踏云头履，立于椭圆形四足底座上。

I. This statue is made in Ming Dynasty, partly colour painting, copper gild. The statue is 64.2cm high and 18.6kg weight. He wears small helmet with red hair and red beard. He wears armour and short robe outside. He holds a weapon(the weapon lost). He stands on the four-foot base with caliga.

II. This statue is made in Ming Dynasty, partly colour painting, copper gild. The statue is 65.5cm high and 17.4kg weight. He wears hat with hair and beard scattered. He wears armour and short robe outside. His left hand makes a fist put beside his waist and right arm bends holding a weapon(the weapon lost). He stands on the four-foot base with caliga.

III. This statue is made in Ming Dynasty, copper gild, partly colour painting, 64.4cm high and 22.9kg weight. He wears the Fa hairpin and armour. He holds tiger-shape seal with fierce facial expression. He wears caliga standing on the four-foot base.

IV. This statue is made in Ming Dynasty, partly colour painting, copper gild. The statue is 66.1cm high and 23.3kg weight. He wears hat with loose sleeve long robe. He holds classical book standing on the four-foot base.

V. This statue is made in Ming Dynasty, partly colour painting, copper gild. The statue is 63.1cm high and 21.2kg weight. He wears hat with hair and beard scattered. He wears armour and short robe outside. His left hand holds a Taoist instrument and right arm bends holding a weapon seems beating something. He stands on the oval shaped base.

【风神】

明，铜铸鎏金，通高61.5cm，重14.1kg。该风神站像头戴幞头巾，面部狰狞，身着铠甲，两肩做飞飘（飘带残），左臂前屈手持风轮，右臂扬举执械（械佚），脚踏战靴，呈八字形站立于四细高足方形底座上。

风神，亦称风伯、风师。道教认为，风伯为天帝下属的神祇，其作用有二：一是受天帝命令刮风或息风；二是为天帝的信使。其信仰起源甚早，《山海经大荒北经》载："蚩尤作兵，伐黄帝。请风伯、雨师，纵大风雨。"春秋战国以后，风神信仰逐渐统一，中原一带信仰的风神为星宿，南方一带信仰的风神则为鸟形或带有羽翼的飞廉（中国神话中的神兽）。秦汉以后，道教吸收了这一信仰，列风神入神系，将二者信仰进行统一。风雨雷电是先于人类而存在的大自然现象，人类对其充满了神秘和恐惧感，认为这种现象即是神在支配，于是将这些现象神格化，产生了风伯雨师雷公电母的崇拜。

The wind deity

This statue is made in Ming Dynasty, copper gild, 61.5cm high and 14.1kg weight. This standing statue of Aeolus wears a kind of head-cover with ferocious facial expression and wearing armour. The flying ribbon on his shoulder (the ribbon lost). His left arm bent before holding the wind wheel and right arm lift up holding weapon (the weapon lost). He wears caliga standing on the square base.

The wind deity is also called the wind uncle or the wind master. Taoism believes that the wind uncle is the subordinate deity of the heaven emperor. It has two functions: one is to create and cease the wind under the order of the heaven emperor; the other is to be the messenger of the heaven emperor. This belief could be dated back to a very early era. In *The Da Huang Bei of The Shan Hai Jing*, it said that "when Chiyou fought against the Emperor Huang, he invited the wind uncle and the rain master to help him, and then the strong wind and heavy rain came". After the Spring and Autumn period and the Warring States, the beliefs for wind and rain gradually unified. The wind deity worshiped by people in the central plains is the constellation, and the one worshiped by people in the South is the bird-shaped or winged feilian (a supernatural beast in the Chinese legend). After the Qin and Han Dynasties, Taoism absorbed this belief and added the wind deity into the deity system, unifying these two kinds of belief. The wind, rain, thunder, and lightning are the natural phenomena existing before the human beings' presence, so human beings think it mystical and horrific, considering that this kind of phenomenon is controlled by deity. Therefore, these phenomena were deified, and then came the worship for the wind uncle, the rain master, the thunder father, and the lightning mother.

【雷神】

明，铜铸鎏金，通高50.2cm，重12.1kg。该雷神站像头戴筒形帽，身着铠甲，外系短袍，两肩做飞飘，左手持环，右臂扬举小锤，脚踏战靴，呈八字形站立于椭圆形底座上。雷神又称雷公或雷师，古代神话传说中的司雷之神。传说雷公和电母为一对夫妻。雷公一名始见于《楚辞》，因雷为天庭阳气，故称"公"。传其初形为兽，或似鬼，或似猪，而以猴形居多。后状若力士，坦胸露腹，背插双翅，额生三目，脸赤色猴状，足如鹰，左手执楔，右手持锥，呈欲击状，腰部悬挂数鼓，击鼓即为轰雷。能辨人间善恶，主持正义，代天执法，击杀有罪之人，所以后来的形象多为人面人足，以表示对其敬重。

The thunder deity

This statue is made in Ming Dynasty, copper gild, 50.2cm high and 12.1kg weight. This standing statue of Thor wears barrel-type hat, wearing armour and short robe. The flying ribbon on his shoulder with his left hand holding the loop and right arm lift up holding hammer. He wears caliga standing on the oval-shaped base. The thunder deity is also called the thunder father or the thunder master, the deity controlling the thunder in the ancient legend. It is said that the thunder father and the lightning mother are a couple. The name, the thunder father, comes from *Chuci*. Since the thunder represents the yang in the heaven, it is named "father". It was first in the shape of the beast, like the ghost or pig, and mostly of like monkey. And then it became strong, showing up its breast and abdomen, winged and three-eyed, with a red and monkey-like face, and eagle-like feet. Its left hand is holding a wedge, and its right hand gripping a wimble, having a ready-to-beat posture. Beside the deity hang several drums, and the beating of the drums means the thundering. It could make a clear distinction between right and wrong, execute the law on behalf of the heaven, kill the guilty party, and uphold justice. Therefore its image is mostly of men's face and men's feet in order to show the respect.

【火神】

明，铜铸鎏金，通高60cm，重20.4kg。该火神站像头戴幞头巾，身着铠甲，两肩做飞飘，左臂前屈持火轮，右臂扬械（械佚），腰间垂悬鲤鱼飘，脚踏战靴，呈八字形站立于三足底座上。火神即火德星君，常手持火轮。汉代即有四方神之说："东方青龙、西方白虎、北方玄武、南方朱雀，天之四灵，以正四方。"古时人们认为南方之神主火。后经历代演变，人们逐渐将火神作为灶神奉祀。武当山至今还保存有较多的火神庙。

The fire deity

This statue is made in Ming Dynasty, copper gild, 60cm high and 20.4kg weight. This standing statue of the God of fire wears a kind of head-cover wearing armour with the flying ribbon on his shoulder. His left arm bent before holding the fire wheel and right arm lift up holding weapon. There is ribbon on his waist. He wears caliga standing on the tripodia base. The fire deity is the Huode xingjun, holding the fire wheel in his hands. In the Han Dynasty, there was the legend of the four direction deities, "the cyan dragon in the east, the white tiger in the west, the xuanwu in the north, and the red phoenix in the south, and they are the four ling animals which can guide the four directions". In the ancient times, people thought that the deity in the south mainly controls the fire. Then with the time passing by, people gradually sacrifice the fire deity as the stove deity. Until now, there are still many fire deity temples in Wudang Mountains.

【老子传道组像】

明,木质。老子站像通高84.7cm,重9.5kg。头戴纶巾,两耳垂大,弓眉垂目,两腮丰满,双唇紧闭,长须垂于胸前。身穿广袖对襟镶边长袍,右臂平伸于胸前(右手残佚),左手垂放于袖内。外袍于胸前打一十字结,腰系宽腰带,脚穿云履立于卷云底座上,通体木雕贴金。

学道弟子站像通高88cm~89cm不等,重均9kg左右。部分站像头戴髻冠,部分头戴莲花冠。这些学道弟子站像均双耳垂大,脸面丰润,眼睛垂视,双唇紧闭。内穿右衽窄袖长袍,外套广袖开胸长袍,双手十字交叉捧朝笏于胸前。长袍内套裙衫,腰系宽腰带,脚均穿云履,底座亦均雕刻卷云纹饰。全组造像共13尊,为武当山现存唯一的老子传道组像。

该组造像均为木雕贴金质地,人物比例适中,人物面部表情、姿态、衣饰等雕刻线条简洁流畅,表现细腻。整组造像中,老子讲道、传道,弟子闻道、学道,老子传道和蔼可亲,弟子学道神情凝重,犹如一幅立体的传道、闻道图。

The serial statues of Laozi preaching

They are made in Ming Dynasty, wooden. The standing statue of Laozi is 84.7cm high and 9.5kg weight. He is wearing Lun hat and large ears, round cheek with mouth closed and long beard before the chest. He wears loose sleeve long robe. His right arm lift before chest (right hand lost) and left hand hide in the sleeve. The outside robe has cross and wide belt in the waist standing on the pedestal decorated with auspicious cloud.

The students standing statues are 88-89cm high and about 9kg weight. Some are wearing Ji hat and some are wear lotiform hat. The statues are all have large ears and clear face with eyes looking mouth closed. They wear narrow sleeve long robe inside and loose sleeve long robe outside with hands cross holding Chao Hu before chest. The pedestals are decorated with auspicious cloud. The 13 statues are the only serial statues of Laozi preaching preserved in Wudang Mountain.

This series of statues are all the gild woodcarving group statues with moderate figure proportion. Their facial expression, gesture and clothes are all carved carefully and fluent. Laozi's preaching and his students' listening seriously are forming a solid preaching-and-listening scene.

【铜铸鎏金灵官站像】

明，铜铸鎏金，通高均为27cm，重均为0.9kg。两站像均头戴翼善冠，内着铠甲，外罩短袍，左手扶于腰际，右臂前曲执鞭（鞭佚），脚踏战靴，立于三足底座上。

The copper gilding Ling official standing statue

This two statues are made in Ming Dynasty, copper gild with the height of 27cm and 0.9kg. Both of the statue are wearing Yishan Hat, armour inside and short robe outside. The left hand put on the waist, while the right arm bent before chest holding lash (the lash lost). They wear caliga standing on the three-foot base.

灵官是道教中的护法之神，能济世助人，有九地灵官、十天灵官、水府灵官等，后来又出现了五百灵官。五百灵官是根据真武大帝入武当山修道传说而得来，其父静乐国王遣将率五百兵赴武当山寻找，欲请真武太子回国，后这五百兵丁也修道不返，太子得道后便封其为五百灵官，那率领兵丁的五位将官亦被封为五显灵官，也称为"灵官大圣华光五大元帅"。

【铜铸鎏金灵官站像】

明，铜铸鎏金，通高93.8cm，重46.9kg。该站像为道教护法神，头戴武冠，身着铠甲，外罩短袍，左臂屈伸于胸前，面部祥和，似在聆听。该站像脚踏战靴立于卷云底座上，身材魁伟，体态修长匀称。

The copper gilding Ling official standing statue

This statue is made in Ming Dynasty, copper gild, 93.8cm high and 46.9kg weight. He is the protector god of Taoism, wearing the Wu hat and armour and short robe outside. His left arm bent before chest with peaceful facial expression seeming listening. This statue has a beautiful body standing on the pedestal decorated with auspicious cloud.

Ling official is the protector god of Taoism, being able to benefit the mankind. There are nine earth Ling officials, ten heaven Ling officials, and the shuifu ling official, and other names. And then the 500 Ling officials came into being. The 500 Ling officials are coming from the legend of the Great Zhenwu Emperor's cultivating in the Wudang Mountains. Zhenwu's father, the Jingle King, dispatched generals with 500 soldiers to look for him in the Wudang Mountains for purpose of inviting him to return to their state. However, those 500 soldiers did not return, but stayed for practicing. After they successfully practiced into deity, they became the 500 Ling officials. The five generals also practiced Taoto deity, being the five Xianling officials or "the five great huaguang generals of Ling officials".

【铜铸鎏金灵官站像】

明，铜铸，通高70cm，重34.7kg。道教护法神，该站像头戴东坡巾，浓眉曲髯，身着铠甲，左手执环，右手做执械状，腰系垂花如意结，脚踏战靴，造型生动，神态逼真。

The copper gilding Ling official standing statue

This statue is made in Ming Dynasty, copper, 70cm high and 34.7kg weight. He is the protector god of Taoism, wearing the Dongpo hat, thick eyebrows and twist beard. He wears armour with loop in his left hand and weapon in his right hand. There are Ruyi knot tied in his waist. He wears battle boots with vivid posture.

【铜铸鎏金灵官站像】

明,铜铸鎏金,通高148cm,重162.5kg。道教护法神,该站像整体保存完整,双手合握兵械(械佚)。头梳高髻,面目精瘦,全身着铠甲,双脚踏战靴呈八字形站立,右手掌在内,左手掌在外,呈握兵器状于胸口处,嘴唇及下巴有短胡须,头部微偏,斜视前方,双手做演示状。

The copper gilding Ling official standing statue

This statue is made in Ming Dynasty, copper gild, 148cm high with the base, and 162.5kg weight. He is the protector god of Taoism. The whole statue is perservered well and the weapon in his hands (the weapon lost) with hair fixed high in his head with a very thin face. The whole body wears the armour and battle boots standing apart with both feet. His right palm inside and left palm outside form the shape of holding weapon before chest. The mouth and the lower jaw has short beard with head leaning. He looks forward seeming demonstrating of the hands.

【铜铸鎏金持斧灵官站像】

明，铜铸鎏金，通高72.6cm，重23.8kg。道教护法神，该站像通体饰金，部分饰以彩绘，造型传神。其头戴武冠，身着铠甲，外系短袍，左手扶斧形器械，右手掐腰，脚踏战靴呈八字形站立于四细高足方形底座上。

The copper gilding standing statue of Ling official holding hatchet

This statue is made in Ming Dynasty, copper gild, 72.6cm high and 23.8kg weight. He is the protector god of Taoism. The statue is golden decoration and partly color painting with vivid sculpture. He wears Wu hat and armour. His left hand holds the hatchet and right hand put in the waist. He wears battle boots standing on the pedestal.

【铜铸灵官站像】

明，铜铸鎏金，通高98.1cm，重60.3kg。道教护法神，该站像头戴筒帽，怒目圆睁，面部狰狞，内着铠甲，外罩长袍，右手扶于左腕，左手持法器（法器残），脚踏战靴，呈八字形站立于四卷云足底座之上（座局部残损）。造像整体塑造手法独特，头部较小，身材魁伟，造型比例适宜，宛若西方美男。

The copper Ling official standing statue

This statue is made in Ming Dynasty, copper gild, 98.1cm high and 60.3kg weight. He is the protector god of Taoism, wearing the Tong hat, widely open his eyes and armour and long robe outside. His right hand put on the left arm, and left hand holds Taoist instrument (lost). He wears battle boots standing on the pedestal. The carving technique of this statue is very unique, the head is small and mighty body just like the west handsome man.

【铜铸鎏金四臂灵官站像】

明，铜铸鎏金，通高66.3cm，重15.8kg。该灵官站像身长四臂，上两臂高举，左手执日，右手持月，下双臂双手握于右腹前。身着铠甲，外罩战袍，脚踏战靴，面部狰狞，造型生动，栩栩如生。

The copper gilding four-arm Ling official standing statue

This statue is made in Ming Dynasty, copper gild, 66.3cm high and 15.8kg weight. This statue has four arms. The upper two arms lift up holding sun and moon and the other two arms holding before right abdomen. He wears armour and battle boots, serious facial expression and vivid posture, life like.

【铜铸鎏金灵官坐像】

明,铜铸鎏金,通高77.6cm,重22.5kg。该坐像头戴武冠,三目怒睁,面部狰狞,身着明光铠,脚踏战靴,右臂高举钢鞭,作击打状。

The copper gilding Ling official sitting statue

This statue is made in Ming Dynasty, copper gild, 77.6cm high and 22.5kg weight. He wears the Wu hat with three eyes. He wears armour and battle boots. His right arm lift up holding the iron whip seeming to slash.

太和武当
武当博物馆·道教文化展

【铁铸彩绘灵官坐像】

明，铁铸彩绘，通高75.7cm，重25.4kg。该坐像头戴翼善冠，三目怒睁，面部狰狞，右臂高举执钢鞭，腰间悬系鲤鱼飘，脚踏战靴。

Ling official sitting statue of iron color painting

This statue is made in Ming Dynasty, iron, color painting, 75.7cm high and 25.4kg weight. He wears the Yishan hat with three eyes, serious facial expression. His right arm lift up holding the iron whip seeming to slash. There are Liyu belt in the waist and battle boots on the feet.

道教源流·和谐本真

The Original Taoism The Harmonious Idea

道教简史厅
Taoist History Hall

作为中国原始宗教与东方智慧价值的巅峰象征，武当山上千年的历史积淀，体现了中国和谐哲学的基本精神，反映了中国人对健康、快乐、平安、和谐理想的朴素追求。通过对武当道教文化的系统介绍，配合不同朝代的道教礼仪、器物、人物、书画展陈，既是对中国道教智慧价值的感悟，也是对人与自然关系的认真思考。

As symbolize of Chinese original religion and the eastern wisdom value, Wudang Mountain has thousands of years' historical sedimentary deposits which not only concentrated embody the basic spirit of Chinese harmonious philosophy, but also reflects the simple pursue of health, happiness, safety and harmonious. Through the systematic introduction of Wudang Taoist culture, matching with the exhibition of Taoist rites, the implements, the personage, the paintings and calligraphy of different dynasties, it is not only the inspiration of Chinese Taoist wisdom, but also the careful deliberate to the relationship between human and nature.

道教简史厅
Brief History of Taoism

引 言
Preface

　　道教是中国土生土长的宗教，它起源于东汉晚期的"五斗米道"，有着非常丰厚、纷繁的文化基础。自古以来的巫师、巫术、鬼神信仰，以及神仙传说等都是道教萌发的沃土。秦汉之世，社会上读《黄帝》、《老子》、《庄子》成为时尚，老、庄的道家哲学思想影响愈加深广。上述诸多因素，促成了依托道家思想对人生寻求解脱的道教的诞生。

　　《老子》、《庄子》等原是学术著作，但它崇尚的"道"是一种超乎形象的宇宙最高法则，有着神秘的色彩。道教正好籍此将"道"变成绝对的、具有无限威力的"神"，是天地万物的根源。道家宣扬的清静无为、顺应自然及养生处世的思想，也被道教阐发为清静无为、道法自然、长生不老的教理，把《老子》这一道家典籍引为道教的最高经典，而老子也被奉为道教的最高教主"太上老君"。

　　Taoism is Chinese indigenous religion which origin from a religion group named Five-dou-rice in the late Eastern Han Dynasty and based on a rich and profound culture. The necromancers, the sorcery, the belief in ghost and deity and the legend about immortality are all seedbed for Taoist origination and development. In the period of Qin and Han Dynasties, reading the book of *Huangdi*, *Lao-tzu* and *Chuang-tzu* became the fashion in the society. The Taoist philosophy of Lao-tzu and Chuang-tzu has a profound social foundation. All those factors result in the birth of Taoist thought which aimed to seek the extrication from the society.

　　The Taoist works *Lao-tzu*, *Chuang-tzu* etc. are actually academic works, but the notion "Tao" it advocated is a kind of unthinkable image of the highest universe principle which has the color of mystery. Taoism just takes the advantage of this principle to make its "Tao" as a god with absolutely infinite power and as the root of everything in the world. Taoism Thought, which preached the idea of being solitary and inactive, conforming to the nature and regimen, was expounded by Taoist as the teachings of being solitary and inactive, natural Taoist and immortality. Meanwhile, the Taoist took the book *Lao-tzu* as the highest canon and Lao-tzu as the highest hierarch bestowed the honorable title "Taishang Laojun".

【道教神仙图】

　　武当山道教神仙画像，凡宫观皆有，且丰富多彩。它结合中国传统绘画手法，将道教的教理教义巧妙融于其中，集中体现神鬼思想和道士修道生活等内容。元、明时期，道教绘画得到了极大发展。该道教出巡仪仗图绘画技巧精湛。群神的衣冠服饰、仪态神情，以及道教尊神朝礼、出行的仪规，均与人间帝王相似，场面极为壮观。该图中为"真武大帝"，两侧为众神随圣护驾。

Taoist Deity's Portrait

　　Each palace and temple in Wudang Mountain has Taoist deity's portraits which combined the traditional Chinese painting technic and ingeniously added the Taoist teaching to reflect the idea of god and ghost and the cultivated life of Taoist. Chinese Taoist painting further developed in the period of Yuan and Ming Dynasties, the portrait of Taoist ritual procession when perambulate is well expressed the prefect painting technic. The dresses, trappings, manner and expression of those deities are alike to the emperors in the world. So do the manner of Taoist pilgrimage and the ruler of the perambulation. All those scenes are magnificent and spectacular. This picture is mainly about the Emperor Zhen Wu. In both sides, they are the deities who convoyed the Emperor.

道教文化
Taoist Culture

老子 Lao-tzu

道德天尊坐像
sitting statue of Super God of Mortal

道教最高神三清之一，即太清道德天尊、太上老君，位居第三。

Statue of Mortlity God, One of Taoist Three Qings of Super God i.e. Taiqing Super God of Mortal, also called Taishang Laojun, occupied the third official rank among Three Qings.

道教与道家、老子
Taoism with Taoist School and Lao-tzu

【道家】
Taoist School

道家本是秦汉时期的一个哲学思想派别，与道教无关。其学术著作对摄生和对神仙的论述较多，它对"道"的神秘解说以及清静无为、顺乎自然、长生处世的主张都被道教所吸收。

Taoist School is a philosophical faction in the period of Qin and Han Dynasties which had nothing to do with Taoism. Some of its academic works include the concept of deity and immortality. Taoism adopted its mystically explanation about "Tao" and the idea of being solitary and inactive, conforming to the nature and long life.

【老子、太上老君与道教】
Lao-tzu, Taishang Laojun and Taoism

"太上老君"：老子是道家的创始人，道教将他神化，奉为祖师，称为"太上老君"。

道教：道教是神化老子、庄子，吸收改造道家的哲学思想，融合中国传统文化及巫术、养生成仙、鬼神信仰、阴阳五行以及儒学、佛学等理论，在中国本土创立的一门宗教。

Taishang Laojun:Lao-tzu, the founder of Taoist School, was apotheosized by Taoist, taken as Taoist ancestor and given the honorable title "Taishang Laojun".

Taoism: Taoism is the native religion in China with deifying Lao-tzu and Chuang-tzu, adopting and developing the philosophy of Taoist School, combining traditional Chinese culture, sorcery, regime to become immortal, the belief in ghost and god, the Yin-Yang five elements, the Confucianism and the Buddhism.

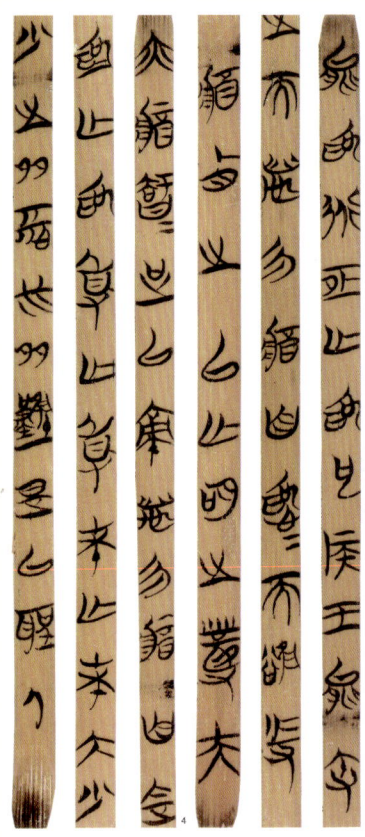

湖北荆门郭店楚墓竹简老子甲（节选）
Bamboo slip from the Chu tomb in Jingzhou, Hubei Province (excerpt)

道家、老子与道德经
Taoist School, Lao-tzu and *Tao Te Ching*

《道德经》与中国思想文化
Tao Te Ching and Chinese Culture in Thought

《道德经》继承了中国古代巫史文化，特别是《易经》、《尚书》等思想并吸收了各地文化传统而成，是一部以"道"为中心的，包括宇宙论、本体论、认识论、方法论、朴素辩证法的哲学体系。老子学说对中国哲学发展有很大的影响，后世很多哲学家都多角度吸收了他的思想。文分"道"经和"德"经两部分，五千余字。

Tao Te Ching is a book mainly about "Tao" including the philosophy of cosmology, ontology, epistemology, methodology and simple diagnostic method. It inherited the ancient mediumistic culture and absorbed the cultural tradition from different regions, especially theories from the book of *Yijin* (also named *The Book of Changes*, a philosophy works) and *Shangshu* (a compilation of historical documents).

《道德经》对中国文学的影响
The influence to Chinese literature from *Tao Te ching*

《道德经》不仅在思想上博大精深，其语言文字如"千里之行，始于足下"、"民不畏死，奈何以死惧之"以及"大音希声，大象无形"等亦成为语句精练、思想深邃的千古名句。

The works are not only broad and profound in meaning but also refined and meaningful in language and words which including many eternal famous phrases such as: thousands of miles walk began from the first step; people are not afraid of dead, why threat them with death.

道教的起源
The Origin of Taoism

张陵 Zhangling

张陵创五斗米道于鹤鸣山
Zhangling established the religion group Five-dou-rice in Heming Mountain

张陵（34～156）字汉辅，沛国丰人，传为张良后代，曾任巴郡江州令（四川重庆），顺帝（126～144）时修道于蜀中鹤鸣山，自称被太上老君授以三天正法，命他为"天师"、"三天法师正一真人"，开始传授五斗米道。

Zhangling (34~156A.D), whose polite name is Hanfu, was said to be the descendant of Zhang Liang (an important official in Western Han Dynasty). He was born in Pei County and once the prefecture of Jiangzhou (Today's Chongqing, Sichuan Province). During the reign of Emperor Shun (126~144A.D), he cultivated himself according to Taoist doctrine in Heming Mountain. He said that he was imparted the Taoist theory for three days by Taishang Laojun and given the title "Tianshi" to him and began to preach the theory of Five-dou-rice.

五斗米道
The Religion Five-dou-rice

五斗米道亦称"天师道正一道"或"正一盟威之道"。据《三国志》、《后汉书》称，道教初创时，受道者需交五斗米，所以这样称呼。特征是崇尚符 、咒祝，令病人思过自首，饮符水等等，是一种有神崇拜的多神教；为人治病，兼以内修，目标是长生成仙。

Five-dou-rice is also named Tian Shi or Zhenyi Mengwei. According to the books of *Brief history of the Three Counties* (Dynasties of Wei, Wu and Shu) and *Brief History of Late Han Dynasty*, in the beginning of this religion, every adherent should turn in five-dou (Chinese ancient weight measurement) of rice. The religion is profound respect for abracadabra and conjuration; aiming to cure diseases for people by letting patients express their penitence for a fault and drink water mixed with burnt abracadabra. It is a kind of mutil-god religion mainly for remedying diseases and self-improvement aiming to immortal and become the deity.

道教的发展
The Development of Taoism

道教与中国名山
Taoism with Chinese Famous Mountains

（一）道教在魏晋南北朝
Taoism in the Dynasties of Wei, Jin and North & South

魏晋时期，朝廷将社会上有影响的方士供养起来，以为朝廷服务。随着道教的发展，道教产生了不同的派别。著名的道士杨羲创立了"上清派"，而葛洪创立了"灵宝派"，江西的葛岭，就是道教"灵宝派"的圣地。

During the period of Wei and Jin Dynasties, the imperial government fended for some influenced Taoists to service the court. As the development of the Taoism, different factions of Taoism came into being. The famed Taoist Yangxi founded "Shangqing" Faction; while Gehong set up "Lingbao" Faction on Geling in Jiangxi Province where the bethel of this faction is.

道教名山——阁皂山
Famous Taoist Mountain—Gezao Mountain

阁皂山，又称葛岭，位于江西省樟树市东南，为武夷山支脉，有99峰，绵延200里，主峰名凌云，海拔800余米。阁皂山风光秀丽，人称"神仙之府"。汉晋时，葛玄及其孙葛洪即在此采药炼丹，布道行医，药界称此山为"祖山"。葛玄在此写成《灵宝秘录》等道教经典并收徒传道，创建了"灵宝派"。

Gezao Mountain, also named Gelin, located in the south east of Zhangshu City, Jiangxi Province, is one branch of Wuyi Mountain and has 99 peaks covering an area of 200 miles whose main peak named Linyun with an altitude of more than 800 meters above sea level. Gezao Mountain has the most beautiful natural scenery and called as the residence of the deities. In the period of Han and Jin Dynasties, Gexuan and his grandson Gehong were here culling herbs for alchemy, preaching Taoism and curing illness. In the field of medicine, Gezao Mountain was called as the father of herbs. The Linbao Faction set here for the Taoist classical works e.g. the *Record of Herbs in Linbao Mountain* written by Gexuan.

道教名山——仙都山
Famous Taoist Mountain— Xian Du Mountain

仙都山位于浙江缙云县，为道教二十九小洞天。道教传说黄帝曾在此炼丹飞升。此地风景绝佳，有鼎湖、孤峰、玉甄岩、小赤壁等名胜。道教宫观有黄帝祠宇（玉虚宫）、黄龙寺、栖真寺、妙庭观等，是人们朝拜黄帝的圣地。

Xian Du Mountain, located in Jin Yun County, Zhe Jiang province, is the twenty-ninth Taoist place suitable for deity living. Taoist once said the HuangDi once came here for self-cultivation and ascended to the heaven becoming a deity. The mountain has the wonderful scenery including some famous key points of interest such as: Ding Lake, Lone Alp, Yuzhen Rock, and Small Chibi. The Taoist palaces and temples are Huang Di Palace (Yuxu Palace), Yellow Dragon Temple, Xizhen Temple, Miaoting Temple etc. which are the holy land for people to worship the HuangDi.

阁皂山
Gezao Mountain

仙都山
Xian Du Mountain

青城山天师洞
Tianshi Cave in Qingcheng Mountain

（二）隋唐北宋道教的发展
The development of Taoism in the Dynasties of Sui, Tang and North Song

隋文帝崇信道教，开国年号就与道教典故"开皇"有关。唐太宗因得道士帮助，登基后抑佛扬道，更称老子是其先祖。宋徽宗崇道为甚，使道教发展到了又一高峰期。

The Emperor Wen of Sui Dynasty, who believed in Taoism very much, named the first year of his reign "Kaihuang" which came from one of the Taoist allusions. Emperor Taizong of Tang Dynasty advocated Taoism because of the help from the Taoists. After he began his reign, he ordered to support and develop Taoism but restrained Buddhism and even took Lao-tzu as his ancestor. Emperor Huizong of Song Dynasty especially worshipped Taoism which makes Taoism come to another most prosperous stage.

道教名山——四川青城山
Famous Taoist Mountain—Qingcheng Mountain in Sichuan Province

青城山亦名天谷山，位于四川省灌县西南，因山形如城，青翠葱茏，故又称青城山。主峰海拔1600米，道教称"第五洞天"。相传东汉道教创立者张陵曾在此修道。之后，晋范长生、隋赵昱、唐杜光庭等高道均在此修炼。

Qingcheng Mountain, known as Tiangu Mountain located in the south west of Guan County, Sichuan Province. The Mountain looks like a city and its woods are very green, thus, people called the Mountain as Mountain Qingcheng whose main peak has as altitude of 1600 meters above the sea and titled as the fifth place suitable for deity living. It's said that Zhanglin, the founder of Taoism in Han Dynasty, once came here for cultivation. Later, many distinguished Taoists were cultivated here, such as:Fan Changsheng in Jin Dynasty, Zhaoyu in Sui Dynasty and Du Guangting in Tang Dynasty.

正一派、上清派、灵宝派的传播
Dissemination of Zhengyi Faction, Shangqing Faction and Lingbao Faction

正一道即天师道。自张陵之孙张鲁去世后，道教向江东发展，形成了以江西龙虎山为中心的符箓派新天师正一派，属张天师后裔所承续，因龙虎山而称之为天师道龙虎宗，其后世代传承。

A religion named Zhengyi was also called Tianshi. Taoism developed to the east reaches of Yangtze River after Zhangling's grandson Zhanglu died, so it formed Fulu faction, New Tianshi Zhengyi faction, centralized by Longhu Mountain in Jiangxi Province. It was continued by the posterities of Zhang Tianshi, and it was called Tianshi religion group Longhu clan for Longhu Mountain, and was inherited generation after generation.

道教天师宗——江西龙虎山
Taoism Tianshi Clan — Longhu Mountain in Jiangxi Province

龙虎山位于江西省贵溪县西南，由龙、虎二山组成，海拔200米左右，道教称"第三十二福地"。道教创立者东汉张道陵第四代孙张胜移居于此，是其子孙世居之地，也是道教"正一派"的发源地。山东南4里处有上清镇、上清宫遗址，为全国风景名胜地。

Longhu Mountain is located in south west part of Guixi County, Jiangxi Province; it is composed by Dragon and Tiger Mountains with an elevation about 200 meters, and was called as the 32nd Fairyland by Taoism. Taoism founder, Zhang Daoling of Eastern Han Dynasty, his grandson of the fourth generation Zhangsheng migrated here, where his posterities lived here generation after generation, and it was also the original place of Taoism Zhengyi Faction. It preserved the relics of Shangqing Town, Shangqing Palace, four miles from southeast mountain and were recognized as scenic spots of national-level.

龙虎山天师府天师殿
Tian Shi Temple in Tian Shi Mansion of Longhu Mountain

白云观牌坊
Memorial Torii of Baiyun Temple

道教的全真派
Quanzhen Faction of Taoism

全真道由金代王重阳（1112~1170）创立，主张佛、道、儒三教平等合一，向南方传播之后吸纳了大批南宗全真派，形成了全国统一的全真派，与合流之后的正一道形成两大派别。

A religion named Quanzhen was founded by Wang Chongyang of Jin Dynasty (1112-1170). It advocated that the Buddhism, Taoism and Confucianism should share an equal position and combined in one. It absorbed a great number of Nanzong Quanzhen Faction after disseminating to the south, and formed national unified Quanzhen Faction, thereby formed two big factions with the religion Zhengyi.

北京白云观
Baiyun Temple in Beijing

白云观建于唐代，又名天长观。金代重建改名太极宫。金末元初，全真道丘处机在此住持，改名长春宫。明洪武年间毁于兵火。现在的规模是在其下院基础上扩建而成，丘处机就葬于观内的处顺堂。白云观是道教全真派十大丛林之一，其庙会在北京久负盛名，是中国道教协会驻地。

Baiyun Temple is built in the Tang Dynasty, also named Tianchang Temple. And it was rebuilt in the Jin Dynasty and renamed Tai Chi Palace. During the late period of Jin Dynasty and earlier period of Yuan Dynasty, Qiu Chuji of Quanzhen Faction was the abbot and renamed it Changchun Palace. During the Hongwu reign of Ming Dynasty, it was destroyed by warfare. The resent scale was expanded on the Down Courtyard. Qiu Chuji was buried in Chushun Hall of the temple. Baiyun Temple was one of the ten big jungles of Taoism Quanzhen Faction whose temple fair had long standing reputation in Beijing. It was Taoist Association station of China.

（三）元、明、清时期的道教
Taoism in Yuan, Ming and Qing Dynasties

元代十分礼遇道教龙虎宗张陵的后嗣，将江南的茅山、天心、灵宝、清微、神霄、东华各道教派别，统由正一天师掌管。

明代皇室崇信道教正一派，朱元璋封天师道教主张正常为正一教主。明成祖朱棣更因道教为他巩固皇权而大力崇拜真武神。

清代康、雍、乾三代对道教均取贬抑政策，道教在朝廷遭遇冷落，地位低下。

The posterities of Zhangling of Taoism Longhu Clan were given extremely courteous reception in the Yuan Dynasty. They put different Taoist factions of Maoshan, Tianxin, Lingbao, Qingwei, Shenxiao and Donghua in Jiangnan district, to be governed by Zhengyi Tianshi Faction.

The imperial family of the Ming Dynasty worshiped Taoist Zhengyi Faction. Zhu Yuanzhang entitled Tianshi Taoist master Zhang Zhengchang as Zhengyi Master. Chengzu Zhu Di of the Ming Dynasty worshiped Emperor ZhenWu for Taoism was very useful in consolidating his imperial authority.

The three generations Kang, Yong and Qian in the Qing Dynasty adopted belittled policy to Taoism. So it was desolated in the royal government and in low position.

道教茅山宗——江苏茅山
Taoism Maoshan Clan —— Maoshan in Jiangsu Province

茅山原名曲山，位于江苏省西南部，地处句容、金坛、溧水、溧阳四县边界，海拔200～300米，主峰髻山、大茅峰分别高410米、330米。道教称第一福地第八洞天。相传西汉茅盈、茅固、茅衷三兄弟在此修道成仙，称"三茅真君"，故名三茅山，简称茅山，道教茅山派即发祥于此。茅山派原称上清派，亦称茅山道，南朝陶弘景在茅山创立，是道教著名派别，主修《上清经》，兼修《灵宝经》。

The former name of Maoshan is Qushan which located in south west of Jiangsu Province, and it is in the boundary of four counties: Jurong, Jintan, Lishui and Liyang, with an elevation from 200 to 300 meters. The main peak Jishan and Damao Peak are 410 and 330 meters in height respectively. Taoism called it the first Fairyland and the eighth Paradise. It's said that the three brothers Mao Ying, Mao Gu and Mao Zhong in Western Han Dynasty, cultivated themselves according to religious doctrine and finally became immortals. They were called "San Mao (the surname of the three brothers) Zhenjun", so it got the name Sanmao Mountain, in short, it was Maoshan, Taoism Maoshan Faction was originated here. The former name of Maoshan Faction is Shangqing Faction, and also named a religion Maoshan Which is founded in Maoshan by Tao Hongjing in the Song Dynasty. It was the prominent faction of Taoism, majoring in *Shangqing Scriptures*, and also studied *Lingbao Scriptures*.

茅山九霄万福宫灵官殿
Jiuxiao Wanfu Temple of Lingguan Palace in Maoshan

永乐宫三清殿
Sanqing Temple of Yongle Palace

永乐宫
Yongle Palace

永乐宫位于山西芮城县。殿宇宏伟，气势极为壮观，内外宫墙，整体布局如紫禁城。永乐宫龙虎殿、三清殿、纯阳殿、重阳殿等四座主要殿阁内的道教壁画极为精美，而三清殿中的"朝元图"更是其中的艺术精华，是中国元代壁画的杰作。现在的永乐宫，系因黄河工程淹没原址而整体迁建的，其工程之浩大，迁建之成功，世所罕见。

Yongle Palace is located in Ruicheng County of Shanxi Province. The palace is grand, with magnificent imposing manner. Its inside and outside of the palace and the whole layout are alike the Forbidden City. Taoism pictures in the four main palaces Longhu Palace, Sanqing Palace, Chunyang Palace and Chongyang Palace, are exquisite. However, the picture of Chaoyuan in Sanqing Palace is the essence of cultural relics and it is the masterpiece of paintings of Yuan Dynasty in China. The resent Yongle Palace is rebuilt on a new site, because Yellow River Project submerged its original place. It is rare in the world for its grand project and successful rebuilt.

三清殿北壁西段朝元图
Mural painting about paying respects to the emperor on the north wall of Sanqing Palace

道教仙境——武当山
Taoist Fairyland——Wudang Mountain

武当派尊崇真武（玄武）。唐代已出现玄武在武当修行的传说。据考证，武当山最早的道教建筑是始于唐代的五龙祠，又被封为道教第九福地。御敕后，历代皇帝嘉封、崇祀、推崇，使武当山逐渐成为中国道教活动中心。

Wudang Faction worshiped Emperor Zhenwu (Xuanwu). It is said that Emperor Xuanwu cultivated in Wudang Mountain during the Tang Dynasty. According to the research, the earliest Taoist architecture of Wudang Mountain was originated from Five-dragon Ancestral Temple of Tang Dynasty, and was titled as "the Ninth Fairyland in China". After that, dynasties of emperors granted it titles, conducted the offerings and worshiped, make Wudang Mountain became the center of Chinese Taoist activities gradually.

道教传播在武当
Taoism Dissemination in Wudang

历代名道云集武当，其中东周的尹喜、尹轨；汉代将军戴孟、马明生、阴长生、叶济；两晋的刘虬、谢允以及姚简、陈抟、房长须、田蓑衣、谢天地、孙元政、吕洞宾、张守清、张士逊等，对武当的发展、鼎盛都做出了极大的贡献。其中南宋的孙寂然在武当山"兴复五龙"，将正一道茅山宗上清派逐步发展形成了崇奉真武、独具武当特色的"五龙派"。

Dynasties of renowned Taoists converged in Wudang Mountain, Yin Xi, Yin Gui in the Eastern Zhou Dynasty; military officials Dai Meng, Ma Mingsheng, Yin Changsheng and Ye Ji in the Han Dynasty; Liu Qiu and Xie Yun in the Eastern and Western Jin Dynasties; Yao Jian, Chen Tuan, Fang Changxu, Tian Suoyi, Xie Tiandi, Sun Yuanzheng, Lv Dongbin, Zhang Shouqing and Zhang Shixun ect. All of them contributed great to the development and great prosperity of Wudang Mountain. Sun Jiran in Southern Song Dynasty "Revive Wulong (five-dragon)" makes Zhengyi religion group Maoshan Shangqing Faction gradually developed to be a unique Wudang featured "Wulong (five-dragon) Faction" who worshiped Emperor Zhen Wu.

五龙宫全景
Panorama of Five-dragon Palace

全真与清微兼容的武当全真道
Quanzhen Faction and Qinghui Faction coexisted in Wudang Quanzhen Religion Group

全真派大家鲁大宥、汪真常来武当率众修复紫霄、五龙等宫观，形成全真派、清微派相融的武当特色教派。

Lu Dayou, Wang zhenchang of Quanzhen Faction came to Wudang, leading the others to repair Purple Heaven Palace and Five-dragon Temple etc, and formed Wudang featured faction, which combined Quanzhen and Qingwei Factions together.

道教鼎盛的武当山
Prosperous Taoism in Wudang Mountain

1418年，永乐大帝赐武当山为"大岳太和山"，位居五岳之上。武当山成为明朝的皇室家庙，宫观建筑、神像、供器与宫廷相望，道团组织为全国之首，武当山道教达到鼎盛，被誉为"天下第一名山"。

In 1418, the Emperor Yongle of the Ming Dynasty entitled Wudang Mountain as "Dayue Taihe Mountain", and it was outstanding above the five famous mountains. Wudang Mountain becomes the imperial temple, its palace and temple architectures, josses, sacrificial vessels faced with the royal palace. Taoist organization was the head in the whole country; Wudang Taoism reached its prosperous stage, and was called "The first famous mountain under heaven".

紫霄宫大殿
Main Palace of Purple Heaven Palace

【铜铸双耳双环宝瓶】

道教供器,明,铜铸鎏金,通高64.7cm,外口径22.2cm,腹径36cm,重28.6kg。宝瓶为直立口,斜颈,肩颈部饰有螭首对称,衔环各一,鼓腹,高圈足,为明皇室御赐武当山宫观的文物精品。

The copper-made vase with two loop handles and two rings

It is a Taoist offering instrument made in Ming Dynasty of copper gilding one. It is 64.7cm high, 22.2cm of caliber, the abdomen caliber is 36cm and 28.6kg weight. Its neck decorating the image of a chi's head (the head of a kind of hornless dragon in ancient folklore) holding a ring in the mouth. It is the precious cultural relic bestowed by royal family of Ming Dynasty.

【莲花双耳双环宝瓶】

道教供器，明，铜铸鎏金，通高126cm，腹径40cm，重59kg。宝瓶整体古朴修长、厚重，瓶口饰以莲花纹，颈部细长，螭首衔环，鼓腹，腹部饰饕餮纹，底部呈六角覆莲状，圈足下六卷云足对称分布。其造型独特、铸造工艺精湛，为御赐精品。

The lotus vase with two loop handles and two rings

It is a Taoist offering instrument, made in the Ming Dynasty with copper gilding one. It is 126cm high, and the abdomen caliber is 40cm and 59kg weight. It is simple, slender, and massy, with its mouth decorating the lotus pattern, its neck decorating the image of a chi's head (the head of a kind of hornless dragon in ancient folklore) holding a ring in the mouth, and its body decorating the taotie (a kind of mythical ferocious animal) pattern. Its base shapes like a hexangular lotus. It is an exquisite article bestowed by the emperor, with unique design and lofty founding technique.

【铜铸烛台】

道教供器，明，铜铸鎏金，通高50.1cm，重17kg。烛台整体分柄、盘、足三部分。长柄中空，托盘敞口外撇，深腹，高圈足。烛台与香炉、宝瓶共称为"五供"，多安放于宫观殿堂之上，为明皇室御赐武当山宫观的文物精品。

The gold-inlaid copper candlestick

It is a Taoist offering instrument made in Ming Dynasty of copper gilding one. It is 50.1cm high and 17kg. It consists of three parts: the stem, the plate and the base. The stem is empty inside. It has been called Wu Gong with the censer and the vessel has been called, usually put in the temples and palaces.

【三足鼎】

道教供器,明,铜铸鎏金,通高55.2cm,口径35.5cm,腹径40.5cm,重46.3kg。盘口,双曲耳,三卷云足,鼓腹,颈部饰有一圈花朵形装饰。鼎在古代主要用于煮食器与礼器,有天子九鼎、诸侯七鼎之礼制,后被道教演化为焚香之用。

The three-leg ancient cooking vessel

It is a Taoist offering instrument, with two loop handles, hoofed legs, and a bouffant abdomen. It is made in Ming Dynasty with the height of 55.2cm, caliber of 35.5cm and 40.5cm body wide, 46.3kg. It is evolved from the ancient cooking vessel. The ancient cooking vessel is mainly for holding the food-containing instrument and the ritual article. There is a ritual system of the emperor's nine ancient cooking vessels and the seigneurs' seven ancient cooking vessels. Later the vessel evolved into the use of censing by Taoism.

【寿龛】

道教葬具，亦称"寿龛"。明，陶质，通高119cm，腹径81cm，重92.7kg。整件器物由冠、盖、缸三部分组成，整体施以黄褐色釉。器身饰以道人、花草等图案，盖中楷书"寿龛"二字。

寿龛一般为陶瓷烧制，外饰各种吉祥图案，表面施釉。道士在弥留之际由其门徒将其以盘坐姿势装入缸内，待羽化后，再封龛择吉日安葬，有身份的道士再于缸外以砖石建塔、立碑。

The shou shrine

It is a burial instrument, usually made of pottery decorating various auspicious patterns outside, and the surface is glazed. This one is made in Ming Dynasty with the height of 119cm, and the abdomen caliber is 81cm wide and 92.7kg. It is composed by three parts: the head, the cover and the body. The whole shrine is yellow glazed with pattern of Taoist priest, flowers and plants and write the name with regular script.

The shrine is usually made in ceramics with various auspicious patterns and glazing on the surface. When the Taoist passing away, his body will be put into the shrine in a hunkering posture, and then it will be buried in an auspicious day and those high-class Taoists will build the brick-made towers and gravestones.

【青花瓷香炉】

道教供器，清代江西信士捐奉。该青花瓷香炉通高17.8cm，口径23.3cm，重2.4kg。整体为直立口，平底，器身饰以人物、山水、树木等图案。原供于武当山朝阳洞纯阳帝君神位前。

The blue-and-white porcelain censer

It is a Taoist offering instrument, contributed by some believers in Jiangxi province with the height of 17.8cm, 23.3cm of caliber and 2.4kg weight. It is the upright mouth and flat base with the decoration of patterns such as statues, mountain and water, woods. It is originally use of worshiping the Chunyangdijun in the Chaoyang Cave in the Wudang Mountains.

【青花瓷供炉】

道教供器，明代御赐。通高47.2cm，重9.5kg。平口方颈，双耳（耳佚），腹部微鼓，四足外侈，正反分别绘有双龙戏珠、双凤朝阳、山水人物以及缠枝莲纹等图案，其画工精细，烧造精良。

The blue-and-white porcelain offering censer

It is a Taoist offering instrument, made in Ming Dynasty with the height of 47.2cm, and 9.5kg. It has loop handles and has flat form. The front and the back are both decorated with the image of two dragons playing with a bead and two phoenixes' leaning towards the sun, as well as mountains, water, people, and the pattern of tangled branches. It is of exquisite painting and fine making technique.

【铜花觚】

道教供器，清，铜质，通高34.3cm，口径10.5cm，重2.85kg。喇叭口，细颈，球腹，方形底做对称四足。质地分铜、木、瓷不等。花觚始于元代，主要流行于明嘉靖、万历至清乾隆时期。早期的花觚除了陈设之外，民间多用于插花，布置厅堂，人们通常把花觚描述为"尊"。经过明嘉靖、万历两朝的发展，花觚的造型也更加多样化。花觚造型隽秀，端庄大方，线条变化十分丰富。装饰题材丰富多样，有人物故事、民间传说、花卉虫鸟等。花觚的时代特征十分明显，明代的花觚主要为三段式，上面是喇叭口，中间是鼓腹，下部是凤尾，器型古朴典雅，造型优美。

The copper flower gu (goblet)

It is a Taoist offering instrument, made in Qing Dynasty with the height of 34.3cm, 10.5cm of caliber and 2.85kg. The flower gu has different quality, copper, wood, and porcelain, and with different designs. The flower gu existed from the Yuan Dynasty, and became popular during the period from the reign of Ming Jiajing and Wanli to the reign of Qing Qianlong. The early flower gu was mostly used for ikebana and the hall decoration by the civilian besides displaying. At that time, people usually called it "zun". After its development during the time period of the reign of Ming Jiajing and Wanli, it got more diversified forms. It is refined, elegant, and of profuse line changes. There are plenty of decorative themes, such as the story of some persons, the folklore, flowers, birds, and so on. The flower gu has a very obvious feature of that era. The one in the Ming Dynasty mainly contains three parts, the upper the bell-mouthed opening, the middle the bouffant abdomen, and the lower the tail of phoenix. It is quite simple, elegant, and exquisite.

【错金木雕蜡台】

道教供器，明，木质，通高64.9cm，重1.7kg。蜡台整体上下对称，分柄、盘、腹、足四部分。柄为圆柱形，四方敞口，肩颈部四面镂空，球腹饰道教暗八仙图案。该木雕蜡台造型优美，雕刻细腻，上下均饰雷纹，中饰暗八仙和四连方"卍"字纹，并有部分透雕卷草图案。

The gold-inlaid woodcarving candlestick

It is a Taoist offering instrument, wood, made in Ming Dynasty with the height of 64.9cm and 1.7kg. It is vertically symmetrical, consisting of four parts: stem, plate, belly and base. The stem is cylinder-shaped. This candlestick is elegant design and exquisite carving technique. The upper part and the lower part both have the thunder pattern. The middle part is decorated with the pattern of the eight Taoist treasures and the "卍", partly carved the rolled-grass pattern by the openwork carving technique.

【武当山玄天上帝圣牌】

明嘉靖三年（1524）景德镇官窑烧制，并御赐至武当山南岩宫供奉。圣牌顶部为如意头形，牌身为鼓形，斜底，通高99.5cm，重37.55kg，分额、身、须弥座三部分。瓷质釉色为五色，以黄绿蓝为主色，素雅大气，称"素三彩"。圣牌以透雕、镂雕、浮雕三种工艺同时表现，更显玲珑剔透。整座圣牌为七部分组成，上部五件、底座二件。底座呈束腰须弥座形。圣牌下部饰双凤朝阳，双凤呈展翅翱翔云天状。牌位中间蓝地白字，楷书"武当山玄天上帝圣牌"九字，端庄典雅，两侧饰四条腾龙于瑞云之中，上部饰以坐龙图案，犹如"玄"字，形成五龙捧圣，寓意真武修真于南岩宫，在南岩宫飞升崖经五龙捧圣得道成仙。该圣牌艺术价值极高，是景德镇官窑烧制的上乘之品。

The sacred card of the Xuantian Heaven Emperor in the Wudang Mountains

It is bestowed to the South Crag Palace in the Wudang Mountains in the third year of Jiajing's reign (1524 A.D.). This card is composed of three parts: Ruyi shaped head, drum typed body and bevel base with the height of 99.5cm and 37.55kg. It is made of porcelain, possessing five colors. Yellow, green, and blue are the main colors, called the "the elegant three colors". The card possessing the openwork carving technique, the through-carved work technique, and the relief sculpture technique at the same time, so exquisite. The whole sacred card is composed of seven parts: five in the upper, and two in the base. The base has a shape like the shuyao xumi pedestal. The lower part is decorated two phoenixes' leaning towards the sun, spreading the wings, and getting ready for flight. In the middle, there are some white words on a blue background, "the sacred card of the Xuantian Heaven Emperor in the Wudang Mountains" in the regular script, so elegant. On the side, there are four dragons above the auspicious cloud. In the upper part, there is a sitting-dragon pattern, like the shape of the word Xuan. Then the image of five dragons' holding the sacred card is formed, representing that Zhenwu was practicing in the South Crag Palace, then he flied from the South Crag Palace, and finally he became deity through the holding of the sacred card by five dragons. This sacred card has an extreme high artistic value, being the high-class article made in the official stove in Jingdezhen.

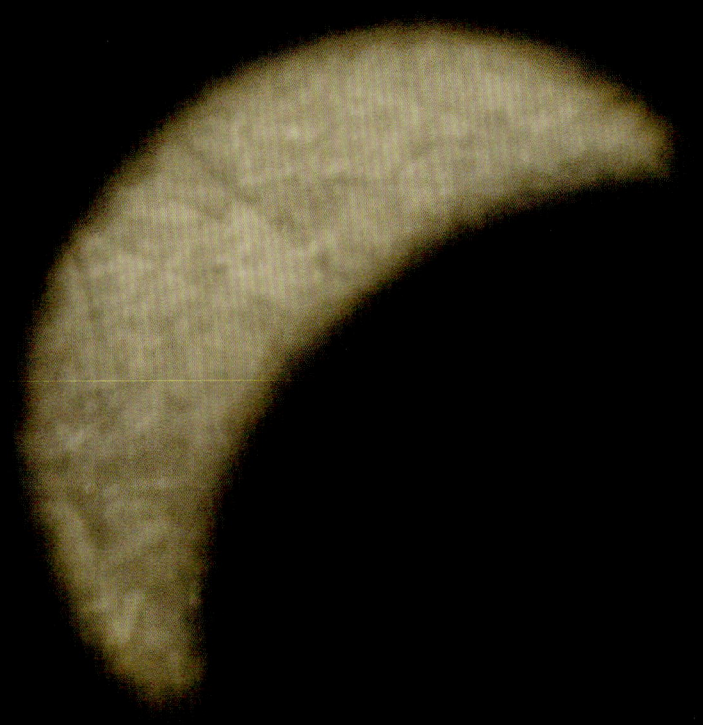

【七星莲花灯】

道教供器，明，铜质，通高87cm，重5kg。该莲花灯制作考究，灯盘呈六边形，上层有六条龙首装饰；中部饰钱纹镂空太极球，灯台为七朵仰莲，并穿一只莲藕，专供上蜡使用；下层为六足镂空底座，饰雷纹；底盘周饰镂空"卍"字纹。悬挂于殿堂内极富道教韵味与祥瑞气息。

The seven-star lotus lamp

It is a Taoist offering instrument made in Ming Dynasty, copper made with the height of 87cm and 5kg. It is made so exquisitely. The lamp panel is of hexagon, with the upper having the decoration of six dragon's heads, the middle having the money-like decoration and a through-carved Tai chi ball, the lower being a six-leg through-carved base decorated with thunder patterns. The lamp holder has seven upward lotuses with a lotus root for putting candles. The border of the base has the through-carved Chinese character "卍" decoration. Hanging it in the hall will add much Taoist and auspicious favor.

【老子骑青牛】
据《史记·老子列传》载,老子见周朝衰败,遂离周西去,至函谷关,为关令尹喜所留,请老子著书,遂有老子五千言《道德经》问世。

Lao-tzu's riding on cyan cattle

According to *The Biography of Laozi in Shiji (The Historical Records)*, seeing the downfall of the Zhou Dynasty, Lao-tzu left the Zhou state to the Hanguguan, and he was asked to stay by Guanling Yinxi and invited to write books. Then his five-thousand-word *Tao Te Ching* came into being.

道教简史厅
Taoist History Hall

道教简史厅
Taoist History Hall 158-159

香俗朝宗 · 福寿康宁
Pilgrimage Brings You Wealth, Healthy, Happiness and Longevity

香俗文化厅
Pilgrimage Culture Hall

　　武当仙山灵，万人赶武当。几千年来，武当山一直被作为道教文化的巅峰圣地而为世人瞩目。尤其是每逢农历三月三真武圣尊等重大道教节日，武当山重要的道观场所都要举行盛大的法事活动，在海内外具有广泛的影响力。武当山庙会已被列入国家非物质文化遗产名录。

　　武当山真武道场，自宋以降日趋兴旺，经元至明，民间真武崇拜的宗教信仰也愈来愈盛。尤其是明代，因明皇室的大力推崇，使民间真武崇拜、朝山进香的民俗活动遍及我国大江南北，北到河南、陕西、山西，西到四川、云南等省。每年全国各地均有大量民间组织的朝山进香团奔赴武当。

Wudang Mountain being taken as the effective mountain, many people come here to pilgrimage. Over thousand years, Wudang Mountain is well-known to the world as holy land for its Taoist culture. Especially, the Taoist festivals such as the lunar calendar 3rd of March, the important temples and palaces will hold right royal activities which have widely influence at home and abroad. Wudang Mountain fair has been list as the national immateriality cultural relic.

The Zhenwu Taoist rite of the Wudang Mountains has become more and more popular from the Song Dynasty, through the Yuan Dynasty to the Ming Dynasty, and so do the civil belief of Zhenwu. Especially in the Ming Dynasty, because of the great advocacy from the royalty, the civil belief of Zhenwu and the civil censing activity has prevailed throughout the whole country, including Henan province, Shanxi province, and Shanxi province in the north, Sichuan and Yun'nan provinces in the west. Moreover, the custom of going to the Wudang Mountains to cense has still been kept until nowadays.

【香客供品】

每年农历道教重要节日，民间香客均要向真武祖师敬奉神冠、披风、寿桃、万民伞、令旗等，其中万民伞最富武当香俗文化特色。因万民伞象征着华盖，意为真武祖师福被万民，护佑着天下苍生，故香客信士在赴武当大型朝会时，均要将自己的姓名做成名签层叠缝置于伞周，且年年使用，从不间断，有些万民伞甚至连续使用上百年。

Offering

Every year when the Taoist festivals, there are offerings sacrificed to the Zhenwu God by civil believers, such as the cop, the peach, the flag, the umbrella for many civilians, and so on, among which the umbrella most has the feature of pilgrimage culture. This umbrella represents wealth and the benefit for all civilians. Every believer writes his name on a piece of paper, and then putting them in cascade around the umbrella and use it every year which even can use hundreds of years.

神冠 celestial hat

寿桃 peach

令旗 flag

万民伞 umbrella

【锁口剑】

清，长9.2cm~16cm不等，有铜、铁两种质地，形状呈宝剑形。

锁口剑为古代信士向神灵许愿的一种酷刑。这种许愿方式一般是为父母久病不愈时使用。信士在赴武当之前，先沐浴更衣，然后用锁口剑刺穿腮帮，沿途杜绝饮食，直到武当山拜见真武祖师许下重愿后，才能取下。等许完愿后，取出剑体，另从金殿香炉内取些香灰抹上即可，至今我们仍能看到这种许愿香俗。

The suokou sword

They are made in Qing Dynasty, with the length of 9.2cm to 16cm. It's usually made of copper or iron, shaping like a sword.

It is a kind of excruciation for the ancient believers to pray to god. This method for praying is commonly used when parents are ill for a long time and do not have the evidence of recovering. Before the believer goes to the Wudang Mountains, he will take a bath and wear some new clothes. Then he will pierce his cheek by that suokou sword, and do not eat or drink anything on the road. Only after he reaches the Wudang Mountains and makes a wish to the Zhenwu God can the sword be taken away and use some incense ashes to wound. We still can see such kind of praying custom until now.

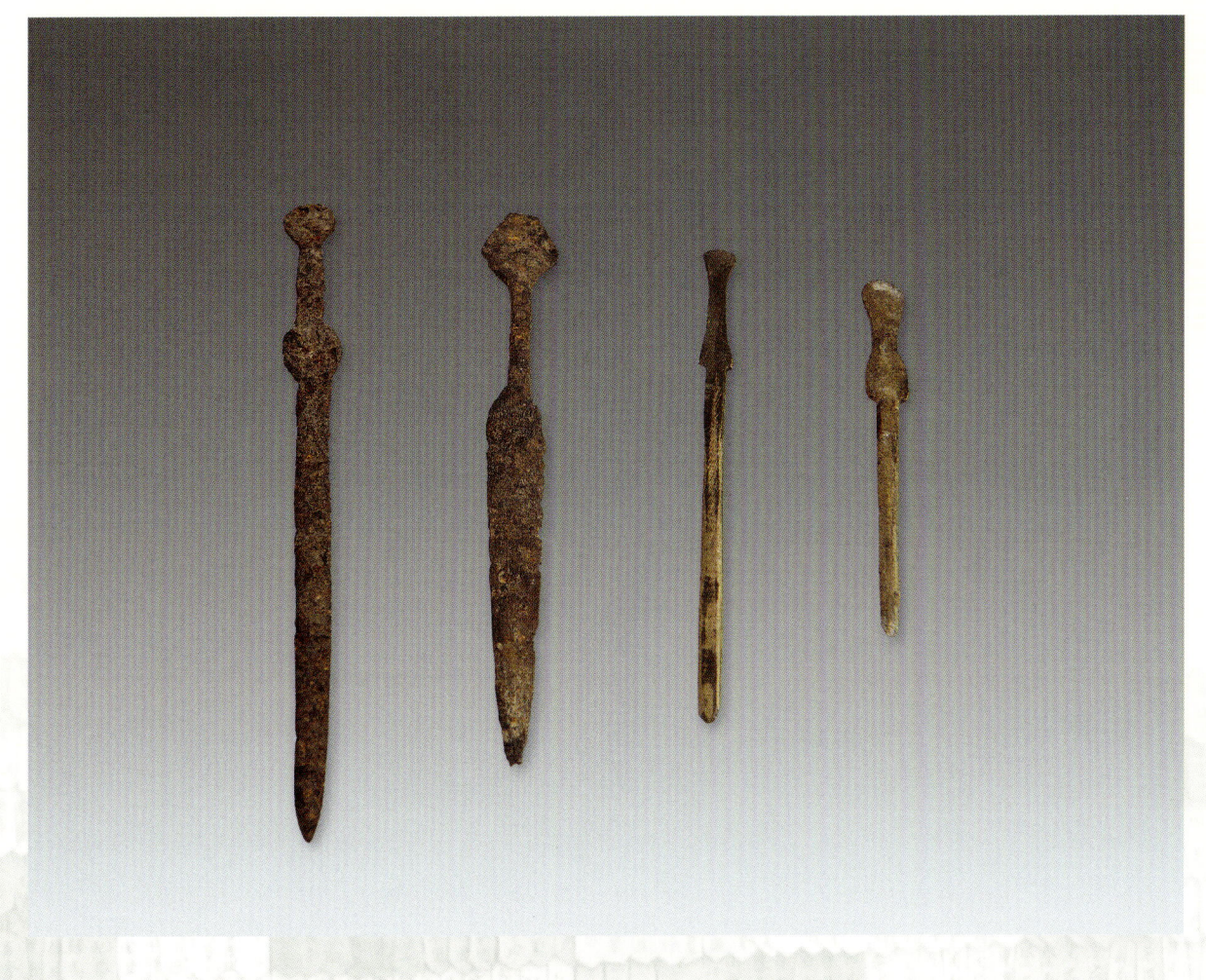

【五百灵官】

　　道教护法神。明，木雕彩绘，通高19cm~22cm不等。五百灵官以王灵官居首，执鞭着铠，十分威武，奉于山门前殿。在真武传说中，真武原为静乐国太子，因舍弃王位到武当山修真，其父静乐国王派官率五百兵将到武当寻访太子，欲劝回国，五百兵将见太子修炼意坚，便跟随太子修真悟道。太子成仙后封五百官兵为护法神，俗称"五百灵官"。在武当山五百灵官的造像中，亦是多种多样，质地有铜铸、铁铸、木雕、石雕等，服饰上也有文武之别。

　　五百灵官之首王灵官，亦称"灵官王元帅"，赤面髯须，身披金甲红袍，三目怒视，左手持风火轮，右手举钢鞭，形象威武勇猛，令人生畏。王灵宫相传本名王善，宋朝人，为人正直，曾从蜀人萨守坚学道，被玉皇大帝封为"先天主将"，司天上、人间纠察之职。道教将其像塑于玄岳门前灵官殿内，用以镇守宫观，注视着进山朝拜的往来信士，恪守自已的言行举止。

木雕彩绘五百灵官站像
wood carved colour painting standing statue of 500 Ling Officials

铁铸鎏金五百灵官
iron gild standing statue of 500 Ling Officials

石雕五百灵官
stone carved standing statue of 500 Ling Officials

The 500 Ling officials

They are the protector gods of Taoism leading by the Wang Ling official who is so powerful, holding a scourge, wearing the armor, and standing at the front hall. Those are made in Ming Dynasty of wood carved painting statues with the height of 19cm to 22cm. In the legend of Zhenwu, Zhenwu was originally the prince of the Jingle Kingdom. He abandoned his status and went to the Wudang Mountains for practicing. His father, the king of the Jingle Kingdom, dispatched generals with 500 soldiers to go to the Wudang Mountains in order to find him and to persuade him to come back. However, the soldiers saw that the prince was so determined. Therefore, they followed the prince to practice. After the prince's practicing into deity, they were conferred to be the protector gods, or "the 500 Ling officials". Those statues of the 500 Ling officials are also diversified, having different qualities, like the copper, the iron, the wood, the stone, etc. You can distinguish the cultural officials from the military officials from each other.

Wang Ling official is the leader of the 500 Ling officials, who is also called "the Ling official and general Wang". He has a red face and whisker, wearing a golden armor and a red robe, three-eyed, looking angrily. It is said that his original name is Wang Shan, living in the Song Dynasty, with an upright character. He has learnt Tao from Sa Shoujian who was from the State of Shu, and he was conferred by the Jade Emperor in Heaven as "the main general of the heaven", taking charge of the picketing affairs of the heaven and earth. Therefore Taoism builds his statue inside the gate to the monastery for guarding the temple. He holds the fire wheel in his left hand and the steel scourge in his right hand. His image is so powerful, brave, and horrific.

铜铸鎏金王灵官坐像
copper gild sitting statue of Wang Ling Official

【朝山泥塑场景】

武当香俗，古今皆盛，上至帝王，下至平民，世代延续。香俗分多种类型，其中尤以农历三月三、九月九最盛。据明张开东《大岳赋》载：武当香客"踵磨石穿，声号山裂"。在香俗中，最虔诚、最残酷的莫过于烧大香、烧苦香，这类香客出发时便用一短剑将脸颊刺穿，沿途不进饮食，待抵武当面圣默祷完毕后，方能取下"锁口剑"。此外还有绝食、许愿、还愿、化缘、积德等多种类型。

scene of the pilgrimage of clay sculpture

The pilgrimage activities in Wudang Mountain are prosperous from ancient time till nowadays which succeeded generation after generation for both emperors and folk people. There are different types of pilgrimage activities, among which the pilgrimage activities on March 3rd and September 9th in Chinese lunar calendar are the most warmly welcomed festivals. According to the description in *Ode to Da Yue* written by Zhang Kaidong in the Ming Dynasty, the pilgrims in Wudang Mountain were great in number and extremly loud in beating and blowing during the pilgrimage precession. In the culture of pilgrimage, the most pious and rigorous behavior of the believers are burning big incense and burning hard incense. Pilgrims in this type use short sword to prick across the cheeks at the moment of departure and eat nothing in the procession. After reaching Wudang Mountain, finishing the pilgrimage activities, they can take out the mouth-locking sword. Apart from that, there are other ways of pilgrimage such as: fast, making a vow, expressing gratitude for successful vowing, soliciting money and doing good deeds.

香俗文化厅
Pilgrimage Culture Hall

凡到武当敬香，出发前须沐浴净身，不食荤腥，带上贡品，身背黄色香袋，胸围黄色衣裙，手持令旗、万民伞等，一路吹拉弹唱，奔赴武当，且沿途纪律严明。香客们由于害怕"灵官爷发怒，将其杖于南天门下"，均不敢逾雷池半步，逢庙必进，见神即拜。

Those who came to Wudang Mountain for pilgrimage, should have a bath and change clothes, not eat meat or drink wine, bring offerings, carry yellow wrappers, dress in yellow and hold the command flags and Ten-thousand-people umbrella ect. The pilgrimage procession beat drums and blew trumpets all the ways to Wudang Mountain with strict discipline. The pilgrims are afraid of being published at the South Sky Gate once they disobey the rules, so they kowtow in each temple and show respects for every deity.

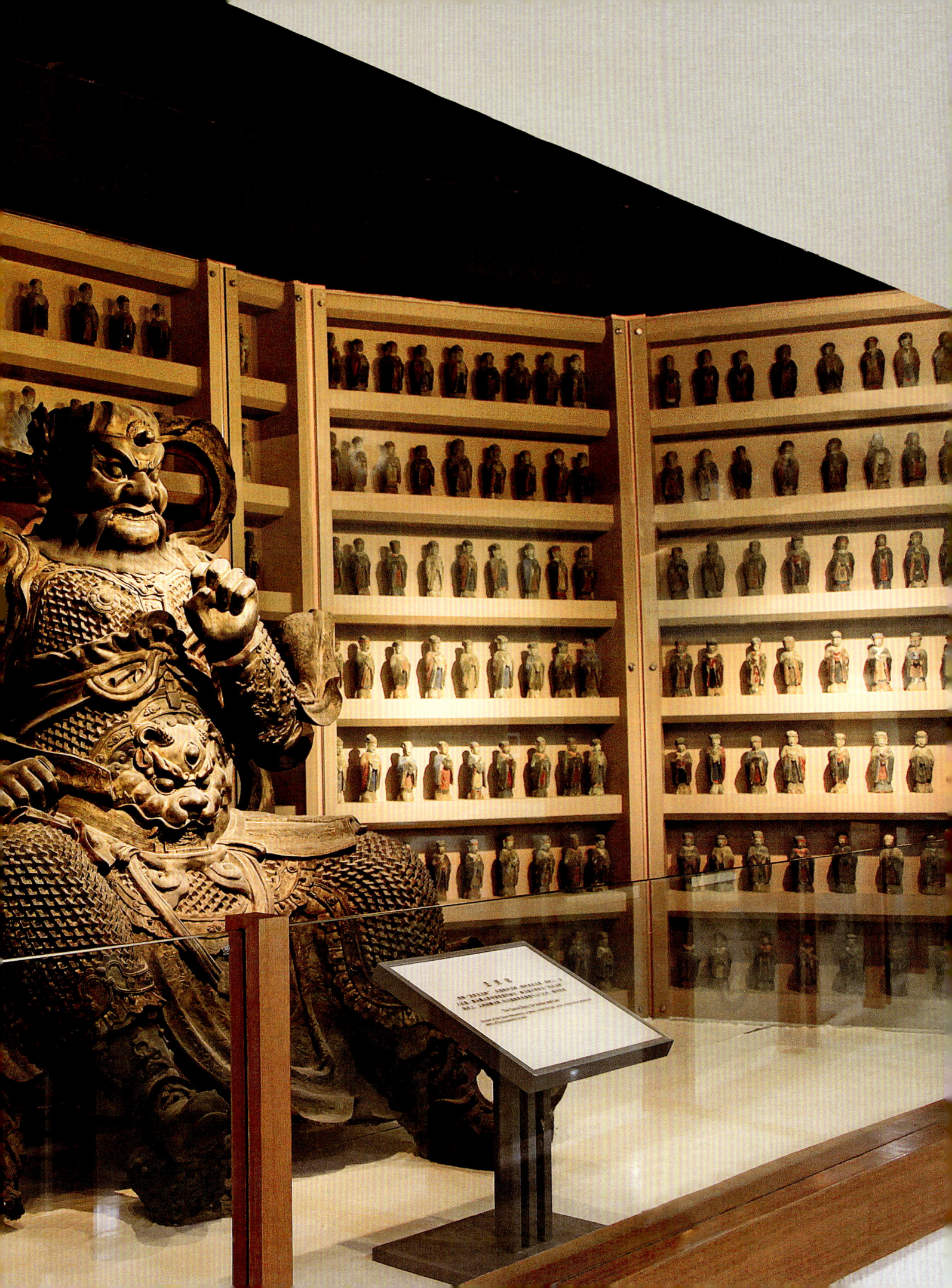

太极祖庭·文明瑰宝
Tai Chi, Cultural Treasure

武术养生厅
Wushu and Regimen Hall

武当武术自古就被尊为武林界的"泰山北斗",素有"南尊武当,北崇少林"之誉。

武术养生厅展出的珍贵文物铜铸鎏金张三丰坐像,是明永乐皇帝御赐。原刻于武当岩洞"秘不外传"的武当武术八大要领,在这里通过幻影成像技术与公众分享。道教武术推拿、裸体男女像、医治跌打损伤的中草药、武术养生所食用的黄精等药材,都是武当太极养生文化的精萃表达。

In the world of martial art, Wudang Kongfu has been highly esteemed as the "great master" since ancient times who enjoyed the parallel position with Shaolin Kongfu in China, as the popular saying goes:"In the north, respects paid to Shaoling Kongfu; yet in the south, honor given to Wudang Kongfu."

Wushu and Regimen Hall exhibits the rarity cultural relic the copper gilding sitting statue of Zhang Sanfeng which is bestowed by Emperor Yongle. The eight key points of Wudang Wushu which has been carved in the Wudang cavity will share with the public through spectra vision. The Wudang Wushu manipulation, male and female naked statues, Chinese herbal medicine of traumatic injury and the medicinal materials which used for regimen, such as sealwort, are all the cream of Wudang Taichi regimen culture.

武术养生厅
Wushu and Regimen Hall

引 言
Preface

　　武当派功夫自古就被尊为武林界的"泰山北斗"，素有"南尊武当，北崇少林"之誉。武当武术以内家功夫名扬天下，具有鲜明的道家文化特征，其内涵博大精深、奥妙无穷，是武术与养生的巧妙结合。武当武术在拳法架势上，注重行圆取象、炼气凝神、不躁不僵；技法上追求内劲充盈、粘随走化、以柔克刚、以静制动、刚柔并济、后发制人。武当武术旨在修身养性，祛病强身；追求身虽动、心贵静、气须敛、神宜舒的无我境界；保持无为、不争、无欲的状态；讲究精、气、神结合；强调先以心使身，而后身从心；用意不用力，意到气到，气到力达。它是一种非常科学、身心训练巧妙结合的特殊运动形式，具有鲜明的内养外炼特征。

　　道教医药与养生学是中国传统医学的一个重要流派。道教出于习医自救、济世利人的目的，向来非常重视研习医药方剂，故形成了崇尚医药的传统。在中国古代的四大发明中，黑火药就是道教方士在炼制丹药时发明的。常言"十道九医"，历代很多道士均精通医术。道教医药源于《黄帝内经》、《周易》及秦汉时期的各种方术，与中医药同根同祖，却又独具特色。医药史上著名的医学家如葛洪、陶弘景、孙思邈等，都是道教医药的重要传承人物。武当山道教医药与养生有着鲜明的地域文化特色。

　　In the world of martial art, Wudang Kongfu has been highly esteemed as the "great master" since ancient times who enjoyed the parallel position with Shaolin Kongfu in China, as the popular saying goes:" In the north, respects paid to Shaoling Kongfu; yet in the south, honor given to Wudang Kongfu." Wudang Wushu possesses a distinct cultural feature of Taoism and is well-known for its Nei Jia Kongfu (Internal Kongfu) with profound connotation and subtle effects. It is a masterpiece of combing Wushu with regimen ingeniously. For its boxing poise, Wudang Wushu lays stress on graceful motion and visual posture, soothing the inner mental state and no temperament or stiffness; for its skill, Wudang Wushu is in pursuit of great strength, defeating the toughness by a tender act, charging the active by still movement, tempering the toughness with gentleness, launching an attack later. Wudang Wushu aims for cultivating the body and character, dispelling diseases and strengthening the body; seeking the selfless realm of body moving with calm mind; maintaining the state of inaction and no desire; insisting on the combination of spirit, mind and strength; emphasizing that body movement should follow the spirit and the spirit can arouse great strength. Wudang Wushu, featured in improving health by regimen and exercise, is a special form of activity subtly and scientifically connecting body exercise with mental discipline.

　　Taoist medication and regimen is one of the most important schools of the traditional Chinese medicine. Taoism aims at studying medicine intensively to cure diseases and provide medicine for people. They always attach great importance to study and practice prescription and medicament. Among China's four great inventions, gunpowder has been discovered by the Taoist in alchemy. People usually say "Nine Taoists who are good at medicine in ten" which illustrate that most Taoists are experts in medicine. Taoist medicine, which has the same origin with traditional Chinese medicine, originated from *Huang Di Nei Jing*, *Zhou Yi* and various remedial methods in Qin and Han Dynasties. In the history of medicine, there have been many famous medical experts who are the heritors of Taoist medicine, such as: Ge Hong, Sun Simiao and Tao Hongjing. Taoist medicine and regimen possess a distinct feature of regional culture.

名震中外的武当功夫
Famed Wudang Kongfu

南尊武当，北崇少林
Revere Wudang Kongfu in South, Honour Shaolin Kongfu in North

武当武术是中华民族优秀的文化遗产，也是武当山非物质文化遗产的重要组成部分。它名震中外，深入人心，不仅利于强身健体，还非常具有观赏性，经常在各类影视中重点展现。

Wudang Wushu is the precious Chinese cultural relics; meanwhile it is an important part of non-material cultural relics of Wudang Mountain. It is warmly welcomed by many people both at home and abroad. It is a kind of sports not only for keeping healthy but also for appreciation, which often appears in various films and TV plays.

张三丰与武当功夫
Zhang Sanfeng and Wudang Kongfu

张三丰是中国古代一位神奇的武功大家，是武当武术的祖师。关于张三丰的传说非常多。他约生活在元代，按其自述为"大元遗老"，到了明初，开国皇帝朱元璋及永乐帝还派专人到武当山等地寻找张三丰，可见他的影响之大。

Zhang Sanfeng is an ancient great master of martial art and the founder of Wudang Wushu. There are different legends about Zhang Sanfeng. He lived in Yuan Dynasty and claimed to be the most influential person in Yuan Dynasty. In the beginning of Ming Dynasty, the first Emperor Zhu Yuanzhang and Emperor Yongle sent people to look for Zhang Sanfeng in Wudang Mountain which showed that he had profound influence in history.

武当武术的经典，都源自张三丰，如纯用内功的"内家拳"——太极十三式、形意拳、八卦掌、太极剑等，均名震中外，且经常在各类武打影视中戴着神秘的面纱出现。

The most essence of Wudang Wushu are derived from Zhang Sanfeng, e.g. Form-and-will Boxing, Eight-diagram Palm and Taiji Sword, which are well-known to the world and appear mystically in different swordsmen films.

武当功夫与影视文化
Wudang Kongfu with Film and TV

电影《武当》
Film *Wudang*

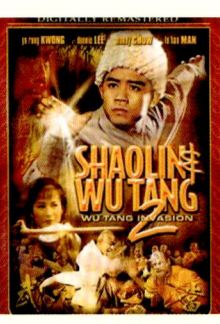

电影《木棉袈裟》
Film *Mu Mian Jia Sha*

电影《太极张三丰》
Film *The Tai-Chi Master*

电视剧《笑傲江湖》
Teleplay *Xiao'ao Jiang Hu*

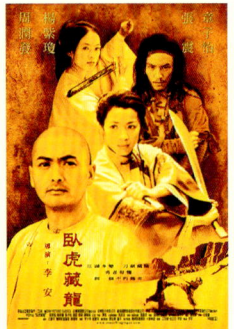

电影《卧虎藏龙》
Film *Crouching Tiger Hidden Dragon*

电视剧《武当2》 Teleplay *Wudang* II

电视剧《倚天屠龙记》
Teleplay *Yi Tian Tu Long Ji*

电视剧《武当1》
Teleplay *Wudang* I

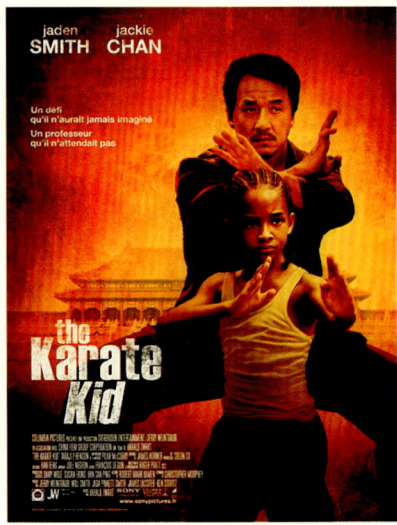

电影《功夫梦》
Film *The Karate Kid 2010*

武当道教与医药养生
Taoist Medicine and Regimen of Wudang Mountain

在继承中国传统医学同时，道家结合自身实践，开创了与传统医学既有联系又独具特色的道教医药学。以葛洪、陶弘景、孙思邈、李时珍等为代表的历代"道医"都为后世做出了不可磨灭的贡献，并留下了许多珍贵的医药文献。道教医药着重于研究养生和炼丹术，它为传统中医学和古代制药工艺做出了贡献，道教养生的发展也有力地推动了中医学及相关科学的发展。

Taoist medicine originally created the distinct Taoist medicine and pharmaceutical with inherited the traditional Chinese medicine, explored human body and based on self practice. Many Taoist doctors, representing by Gehong, Tao Hongjing, Sun Simiao and Li Shizhen, contributed greatly to the late medicine and left a lot of precious medical documents. Taoist medicine attached great importance to research on regimen and alchemy which make contribution to traditional Chinese medicines and the technique of ancient pharmacy. The progress of Taoist regimen also promoted the development of traditional Chinese medicine science and related science.

《本草纲目》与武当山
Compendium of Materia Medica and Wudang Mountain

武当山地处亚热带季风区，气候温润，是野生动植物生长的天堂。武当山药用动植物非常丰富，仅药材就达617种。明代著名医学家李时珍的《本草纲目》中所载中草药，有417种源自武当山。武当道教秘传针灸、按摩、内功疗法等多达230余种，世传膏、丸、锭、丹等中成药近百种，称得上是中国道教医药文化的宝库。近年调查、整理获知，武当山地区共有中草药820余种，其中"蔓陀萝花"、"七叶一枝花"、"头顶一颗珠"、"江边一碗水"等为我国名贵药材。

Wudang Mountain locates in subtropical monsoon zone and its mild climate provides wild life with a good living condition. Wudang Mountain is abundant with medicinal materials and only the medicine-use plants have reached 617 kinds. There are 417 types of medicine-use herbs in Wudang Mountain recorded in *Compendium of Materia Medica* written by the famous medical man Li Shizhen in Ming Dynasty. There are more than 230 kinds of Taoist acupuncture, massage, internal treatment and nearly 100 sorts of medicaments of plasters and pills which are the cultural treasure of Taoist medicine. According to resent investigation and collection, there are more than 820 sorts of herbs in Wudang Mountain, among which there are national precious raw material for medicine, such as stramonium and Paris polyphylla.

武当山珍稀药用植物
Rare Medicine-use Plants in Wudang Mountain

武当道医经过长期观察实践，总结出"本草中容善治风，对枝对叶能治红，叶边有齿能消肿，叶有浆具拔毒功"的宝贵经验。

Taoist medical men summed up some valuable experience through long-time observation and practice that some herbs can cure stroke, some branches and leaves can stanch, some vegetation with tooth-shaped leaves can lessen the tumescence and some leaves with juice can eliminate poison.

武当医学的特色
The Characteristics of Wudang Medicine

一、"四个一"疗法
Four "one" therapies

"一炉丹"（成药）、"一双手"（推拿）、"一根针"（针灸）、"一把草"（草药）。
"one stove" (internal medicine) "one pair of hands" (massage) "one needle" (acupuncture) "one handful of herb" (herbal medicine)

二、医道自采、自制、自用中草药，经长期实践，对中草药药态、药性、配比有丰富经验。

Medicinal herbs are made by Taoists who collected, produced and used by themselves. The Taoists have rich experience in learning condition, nature and usage of the medicine through long-term practice.

三、武当名药
Famous medicaments

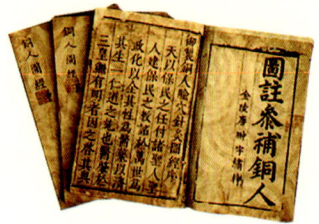 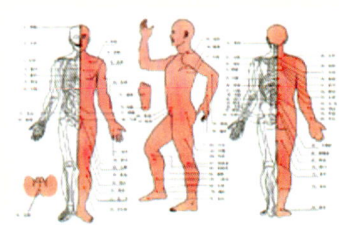 

武当道教医药中的养生学
Regimen in Taoist Medicine

道教医药养生文化的另一内容，是道教的养生修炼学说，其与道教演进的多种因素息息相关。道教的养生、修炼也有信仰鬼神、祈盼飞升的思想，表现在养生方面，自古就有外丹术、内丹学、导引法、辟谷等等。有些方法如外丹术，因历代服食丹药被夺命者难以计数，早已废弃，而主张人与自然和谐、调整自我、摒除杂念、维护心理健康而达到强身目的的内丹、导引等方法，如果运用得当，再辅以一定的肢体运动、科学饮食等，确实对人的身体素质大有好处。这些武当道教的修身、养性理论，是武当山非物质遗产的重要组成部分。

As the other content of Taoist medicinal culture, the theory of regimen and cultivation has the same origin with Taoism. Taoist regimen and self cultivation have the idea of believing in ghosts and gods and hoping to ascend to heaven. In regimen, there are methods such as Wai Dan (external medicine), Nei Dan (internal exercise of the body) and Dao Yin (guiding skills of regimen). Some methods e.g. taking external medicine has been abandoned for a long time because many people died for the external medicine which was the so-called pills of immortality. While some methods such as Nei Dan (internal exercise of the body) and Dao Yin (guiding skills of regimen), which maintain the ideas of the harmony between man and nature, keeping mind and body healthy by adjusting oneself and purifying mind. If this method used suitable and assistant with doing exercises, scientific diet etc., it will really good for physical quality. All those theories of regime are an important part of non-material heritage of Wudang Mountain.

内丹学
Nei Dan (internal exercise of the body)

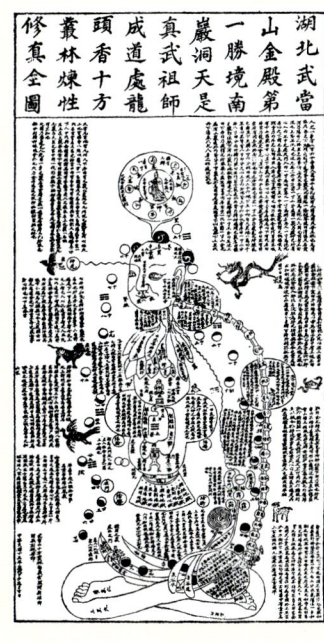

源于行气、导引、胎吸等术。其术将人体特定部位当做丹鼎，炼聚人体的精、气、神而达到"长生"的目的。这种有引导的凝神聚气，对于调力、增强身体活力无疑是一种好方法。

Originated from methods like Xing Qi (Breathing-in & breathing-out skill), Dao Yin (guiding skills of regimen) and Tai Xi (Breath using the stomach), Nei Dan (internal exercise of the body) method means to choose one part of human body with total concentration for resting and relaxing. It is a good way to be energetic and keep in good healthy.

导引术
Dao Yin (guiding skills of regimen)

"导气令和，引体令柔"，这是一种中国独特的气功健身医疗保健方法，其法呼吸俯仰，屈伸手足，使体内血气流通，既需凝神调节呼吸，又需运动肢体，达到"除劳去烦、流通血脉、消除百病、益寿延年"的目的。

Dao Yin (guiding skills of regimen) method is a unique medical treatment using Qikong for body building and health care. It aimed at banishing worries, eliminating sickness and prolonging the lifespan through smoothing the inner mental state mainly by taking deep breath and stretching oneself.

【张三丰组像】

武当山遇真宫旧藏。铜铸鎏金，明永乐十年（1412）敕铸，张三丰坐像通高145cm，重360kg，两侍童通高均150cm，重均187kg。该组造像为铜铸鎏金，面部圆润祥和，刻画生动，栩栩如生，两侍童分列两侧。据明·方升撰《大岳志略》卷三载："铜像西向坐，戴笠，内加小冠。左右侍童二，杖一，扇一。笠径一尺八寸，中外旋揽，如椒眼状，寸约二眼，平布其里，襄汉间呼为斗篷。杖刻龙头，左侍者执焉；扇镂蕉叶，右侍者执焉；皆糜铜以成形，而袭之以金。盖三物，真仙平时所御者也。"

张三丰，辽东懿州人，三丰为其号。以其不饰边幅，又号张邋遢。他在武当山修炼期间，观蛇雀相斗，由此悟通玄机，并结合阴阳五行之原理，创立了以静制动、以柔克刚、后发制人、刚柔并济、"行如蛇、动如雀"的武当太极拳，史称武当内家拳。永乐初年，明成祖朱棣下诏遣使求访张三丰其人，并曾修书一封，书中道"真仙道德崇高，超乎万有，神妙莫测。朕才质疏庸，然而至诚愿见之心夙夜不忘"。但事与愿违，多次诏见而不遇。皇帝甚为惦念，特敕建宫观，命画师画像，范铸其形以奉祀，供人洒扫朝拜，以表诚意。九五之尊的皇帝，为一普通道士铸像建庙，这在中国历史上极为罕见。

武当太极拳被尊为武当内家拳之主脉。太极者，无极而生，动静之际，阴阳之母，练气调神，返璞归真，丹道一体，延寿增智，世人尊之为上古绝学。它以道家理念为指导，以自然为神韵，以养生全形为主旨，以技击为末学，世代传承，经久不息，其动作如行云流水，典雅自然，周身圆润，举动轻灵，沉浮开合，动静相间，以意引气，以气润身，内养外练，心神兼备，性命双修，永享安康。

太极拳常引而不发，无争退让，谦和面世，尊道崇德，于武技一道，亦非身遭危困而不发，发则所挡披靡，无往而不胜。

太极拳法内修外炼，常以推手演练，阴阳互变，弃浊存清，共同提高。太极宗师张三丰将太极拳总结为阴阳五行、八法十三势，现代世间盛行的各门太极拳法，无不以此为宗，故有天下太极出武当之说。

statues of Zhang Sanfeng

They are original preserved in the Yu Zhen Palace, the copper gilding statues made in the tenth year of Yongle reign of Ming Dynasty by the order of emperor. The statue of Zhang Sanfeng is 145cm high, 360kg. The serving children are 150cm high and 187kg of each. They are made of copper and gilded, possessing a kind facial expression, vivid and lifelike. On both sides of the statue are the serving children. According to the historical books, the statue of Zhang Sanfeng sits facing the west, wearing bamboo hat. Besides him, there are serving children on both sides with one holding things for him.

Zhang Sanfeng is from Yizhou in the east of the Liaoning province and Sanfeng is the name he gave to himself. Since he did not care much about his clothing, he is also called Zhang Lata (dinginess). When he was practicing in the Wudang Mountains, he saw a fighting between a pied magpie and a snake, and then he realized the mystery. So he combined with the theory of yin, yang, and the five elements, and created the Wudang Tai Chi which usually called internal boxing. In the beginning years of Yongle reign, Emperor Zhudi gave imperial edict many times which said he want to meet Zhang Sanfeng but never meet him. Then the Emperor Zhudi gave imperial edict to build the palace and make statues according to Zhang Sanfeng's portrayal to show his sincerity that he really want to meet Zhang Sanfeng. It's rare that the emperor built palace for an ordinary Taoist priest.

Wudang Tai Chi is the main one of Wudang Internal boxing. It is subdues the dynamic with the static, overcomes the firm by the gentle, combines the firm with the gentle, surpasses the former. It has been taken as the master guiding by Taoist ideas and mainly aim at regimen and the art of attack coming at last. It continually and naturally likes the cloud floating in the sky and the water streaming in the river, to act both dynamically and statically, cultivated and exercise make both body and mind health.

The Tai chi master Zhang Sanfeng summed up Tai Chi boxing as Yin Yang five elements, eight principle and thirteen postures. The prevailing Tai Chi boxing schools are all base on this. Thus there is a saying that the world Tai Chi come from Wudang.

【太极十三势】

内家拳中的第一代太极拳法由"起势、抱球势、单推势、探势、托势、扑势、担势、分势、云势、化势、双推势、下势、收势"等功防意识较强的十三组动作组成,其中内含吐纳导引、采补、混元桩等三种道家内修养生功法。此外,十三势动作亦是根据锻炼人体八脉的需要所创,而八脉又内连五脏。整个拳法套路,内有五脏八脉,外有五步八法,兼之功防,融合道家养生丹术,故谓"太极十三势"。其动作要领是,虚灵顶颈,含胸拔背,沉肩坠肘,舌顶上颚。练习时,要求形与意合、意与气合、气与神合,六合之中,神形俱妙。动作之中,绵绵不断,如行云流水,松沉自然。动静之中,刚中带柔,柔中有刚,刚柔相合,含而不露,如棉里藏针。呼吸之中,开合自如,升降自然,深细长匀,息息归根。

太极十三势是一种集武术养生为一体的精妙拳法,不但有以静制动、以柔克刚、四两拨千斤、后发先制的武术技击特点,还有发人潜能、开人智慧、充人精神、壮人体魄、祛病健身、益寿延年的独特功效,实为中华武术之瑰宝。

The thirteen postures of Tai Chi

The 1st Tai Chi generation of the Neijia Chinese boxing, composed of thirteen movements with high attacking and defending features, namely "getting up, ball-taking, pushing, stretching, holding, attacking, loading, separating, cloud, melting, double-pushing, finishing and flinching" where three Taoist interior arts, inducing, supplementing and mixture, are included. In addition, the thirteen movements are created according to the needs of the eight pulses which are internally connected with the five organs in the human body. The whole set of boxing is a combination of the five organs and eight pulses inside and five paces and eight gestures outside together with the thirteen postures of attacking and defending. Correlated with the Taoist alchemy, it is hence named "Thirteen Postures of Tai Chi". You are expected, when practicing it, to concentrate your attention, to straighten your back and shrink your chest, lower your shoulders and elbows and lean your tongue against your upper palate. While exercising it, the body, the mind, the air and the spirit should be in accordance with one another and thus the perfect unison of body and spirit is realized. You are supposed to practice it continually and naturally like the cloud floating in the sky and the water streaming in the river, to act both dynamically and statically, making hardness and softness delicately coexist like a needle in the cotton, and to inhale and exhale naturally and in a balance, making every respiration reach the root of the body.

The 13 postures of Tai Chi is a subtle boxing combining the martial art and the health preservation. It not only has the characteristics of subduing the dynamic with the static, overcoming the firm by the gentle, bringing a heavy fist out of a light one, and surpassing the former, but also can stimulate man's potential, develop man's wisdom, complete man's spirit, strengthen man's body, cure diseases, and prolong man's life. It is a treasure of the Chinese martial art.

【武当七星鸳鸯剑】

明，长74cm，剑身宽4cm，双剑合璧，共用一鞘，均铸有北斗七星纹饰，剑柄、剑鞘均为木质，外裹蟒皮，并以铜饰。民间征集，现存丹江口市博物馆。该鸳鸯剑至今仍锋芒毕露，寒气逼人。

wudang seven star mandarinduck sword

It was made in Ming Dynasty, 74cm long and 4cm wide and two swords with one scabbard. The body of the sword has been decorated by the pattern of Charles's Wain. The hilt and scabbard are both wood covered with python skin and copper. collected from folk, now it has been preserved in the Dan Jiangkou Museum. Now the swords are still very sharp.

【拂尘】

拂尘在道门中有超凡脱俗，拂去尘缘之意，是道人云游时随身携带之物。拂尘演练以扫、劈、缠、抖等动作为主，演练起来手飞尘刷，搬、拦、钓、打，含而不露，暗藏杀机。拂尘御敌时变幻莫测，势不可挡，常用来对付敌方高手。

horsetail whisk

In Taoism, the horsetail whisk has the meaning of extraordinary refined and sweeping the destiny. When the Taoist priests roam the world, they often carry the horsetail whisk with him. It is symbolize of rank. The main action contains sweep, split, twine and shake. When defense, it is a good weapon usually used to deal with high ranked Wushu masters.

【青龙偃月刀】

又名"关公大刀"，是《三国演义》中记载的关羽的随身军械，全名"青龙偃月刀"，因刀身饰有蟠龙吞月图案而得名。该刀为明代铸造，原存武当山关帝庙，长213cm，宽50cm，重27kg，通体铁质，刀头与柄连接处的龙头吞口为青铜质地。刀头阔长，形似半弦月，背有歧刃，刀身穿孔垂旄，刀头与柄连接处有龙形吞口。

cyan dragon yanyue broadsword

The broadsword of Guangong is the weapon of Guangong. Its full name is the cyan dragon yanyue broadsword, made in Ming Dynasty and the length of 213cm, wide of 50cm and weighing 27kg, originally preserved in the Guandi Temple in the Wudang Mountain. It is made in iron, the joint of the head and the handle is bronze. The head of the broadsword is very wide and long, shaping like crescent moon. The joint of the sword and the handle are shaping like the dragon bitted the sword.

【剑筒】

道教礼器，原为道教陈设神器之用。道家素有闻鸡起舞的习惯，后来道人多用来存放晨练器械。该剑筒整体通高82cm，口径58cm，重77kg。筒口外侈，斜肩，腹微鼓，器底寰收，圈足外侈。

The tube-shaped sword container

It is a ritual article of Taoism, originally used to hold supernatural instruments of Taoism. Since Taoists have the habit of getting up to exercise when hearing cock's crowing, it was later used to hold morning-exercise instruments by Taoists. The height of the container is 82cm and 58cm caliber with the weight of 77kg.

【灵芝】

中国中医药宝库中的珍品，素有"仙草"之誉。自古以来灵芝就被认为是吉祥、富贵、美好、长寿的象征，有"仙草"、"瑞草"之称，中华传统医学长期以来将其视为滋补强壮、固本扶正的珍贵中草药。民间传说灵芝有起死回生、长生不老之功效。

The glossy ganoderma

It is a treasure in Chinese medicine, honored as "the magical herb". It is related with luck, wealth, goodliness, and longevity from old. It is also called "the magical herb" and "the auspicious herb". The Chinese traditional medicine always regards it as a precious herb for strengthening the body, consolidating the nature, and guiding the rightness. In the folklore, it has an effect of bringing the dying back to health and being ever young.

【八宝紫金锭】

中国自古就有"十道九医"之说，作为中国道教第一名山的武当山也不例外，至今仍流传下多种珍贵药方，"八宝紫金锭"便是其中的一种。八宝紫金锭由200多种珍贵药材配制而成，对治疗幼儿发烧、痉挛等疾病非常有效。

Ba bao zi jin ding

In ancient China, it is said that there will be nine doctors out of ten Taoists. As the first famous Taoism Mountain, Wudang Mountain has no exception, there have been many precious prescriptions left, like the babaozijin pastille which is made of more than 200 precious medicinal materials for curing the infant's fever, the hyperkinesia, and so on.

【木雕裸人】

武当山现存木雕裸人共四尊，其中男性两尊，女性两尊，且年龄不同。原裸体像胳膊、腿均全，且能活动，后均损轶。对于这四尊木雕裸体像，有专家认为与道医针灸穴位、推拿、按摩有关，也有学者认为，道教裸体像是武当内家功夫习练、演示所用，也有人认为是道教"双修派"练功的教具。

中国道教和世界上其它任何宗教的养生有着显著的区别，道家坚信，人是可以通过正确的修炼方法"得道成仙"，从而获得肉体的永生。在这种信念的指导下，他们从来没有停止过对"长生方法"的探索。道家认为，生命的本质是"精"、"气"、"神"，而长生的关键是"练精化气，练气归神"，并衍生了形形色色的不同流派，如"内丹阴阳双修派"。修炼"内丹"是道教修行的重要步骤，只有"内丹"练成，才有可能"丹成成仙"。而"内丹"的修炼方法也出现了两个完全相反的流派"清修派"和"双修派"。"清修派"认为，必须根除欲念，断绝女色，然后才能清心寡欲，精心练"丹"，而"双修派"则反其道而行之，即，"采阴补阳"，认为只有这样才能达到"阴阳平衡"。

道教医药养生文化的另一内容，是道教的养生修炼学说。和道教诞生起源的多种因素相一致，道教的养生、修炼也有信仰鬼神、祈盼飞升的思想，表现在养生方面，自古就有外丹术、内丹学、导引法以及符、辟谷等。有些方法如外丹术，历代口服食丹药被夺命者难以计数，早已废弃。而主张人与自然和谐、调整自我、摒除杂念维护心理健康而达到强身目的的内丹、导引等方法，如果运用得当，再辅以一定的肢体运动、科学饮食等，确实对人的身体素质大有好处。这些武当道教的修身、养性理论，是武当山非物质文化遗产的重要组成部分。

wood carving naked statue

Wudang Mountain preserves the woodcarving naked statues of two men and two women of different ages with rare designs. The legs and arms are all exist and flexible, but later lost. Some people think that this kind of woodcarving naked statues may have some relationship with the acupuncture and the massage of the Taoism medicine. Some scholars consider the Taoist naked statues are used for the exercise and demonstration of the Wudang Neijia Kongfu. And some experts regard the statues as the teaching instruments for the exercise of the Shuangxiu School.

Taoism is an indigenous religion of China, obviously different from other religions concerning about the health preservation. Taoism firmly believes that human beings could become deity through the correct practicing method, and then get the eternal life. Under the guidance of this belief, they never stop the exploration of the way of getting the eternity. In Taoism, the nature of life is "jing", "qi", and "shen". The key of eternity is the transfer among the jing, qi and shen. And from that, various schools are formed, like "the Neidan School practicing both yin and yang". The practicing of "neidan" is an important procedure in the Taoist practicing. Only after the practicing of "neidan" achieves can the turning into deity realize. However, there are two completely opposite schools coming into being regarding the practicing way of "neidan": "the Qingxiu School" and "the Shuangxiu School". "The Qingxiu School" believes that only the desire is eradicated can the practicing of "dan" be realized, while "the Shuangxiu School" just does the opposite, "completing yang by yin" and reaching the balance between yin and yang.

The Taoist cultivatable regimen is other content of Taoist medicine and regimen which is according with the factors of the origin of Taoism. The Taoist regimen and cultivation has also the idea of believe in ghost and god, hoping to ascend to the heaven. For the regimen, there are Wai Dan, Nei Dan, Dao Yin, sign and ward off food. Some methods such as Wai Dan has been banished for a long time because many people died for taking in the Dan. And some are advocated the harmonious between human and nature, through adjusting oneself, eliminate bad ideas and keep psychology health to strengthen body. The way we called it as Nei Dan or Dao Yin, if used properly with some physical exercise and scientific diet which can be good to physical fitness. The Wudang Taoist cultivate theory has an important part of Wudang Mountain non material cultural relics.

1、女裸体像，清，木质，通高63cm，重3kg。该像头部挽髻，面部祥和，体态丰腴，腹部微鼓，双臂、双腿残佚，通体做有底灰。

2、女裸体像，清，木质，通高63cm，重5kg。该像头部披发，慈眉善目，面带微笑，左耳局部残缺，腹部略鼓，双臂、双腿残佚，整体以底灰打底。

3、男裸体像，清，木质，通高123cm，重15kg。该像头部挽发，长耳，面部祥和，身体修长健硕，双臂、双腿残佚，整体以底灰打底，造型生动，惟妙惟肖。

4、男裸体像，清，木质，通高113cm，重12kg。该像头部挽发，面容祥和，额部皱纹神似，两颊深陷，整个面部雕塑出一副老态龙钟的模样，双臂、双腿残佚，整体以底灰打底。

Ⅰ. This wood carving female naked statue has been made in Qing Dynasty, 63cm high, 3kg. This statue has topknot on head. The facial expression is very peaceful with a little bulge on her belly. The arms and legs lost.

Ⅱ. This wood carving female naked statue has been made in Qing Dynasty, 63cm high, 5kg. This statue scattered her hair and a benevolent and kind countenance with smile on her face, a little bulge on her belly. Her arms and legs are lost and left ear partly lost.

Ⅲ. This wood carving male naked statue has been made in Qing Dynasty, 123cm high, 15kg. This statue has topknot on his head and peaceful facial expression. The body is tall and thin. His arms and legs are lost. The whole body is very vivid.

Ⅳ. This wood carving male naked statue has been made in Qing Dynasty, 113cm high, 12kg. This statue has topknot on his head and peaceful facial expression. The wrinkle of the forehead is vivid. The cheek is very thin. He looks very anility. His arms and legs are lost. The whole body is very vivid.

武当道乐·天籁仙音
Wudang Taoist Music Celestial Melody

宫观道乐厅
Taoist Music Hall

在武当博物馆，亲耳聆听武当道家仙乐，感悟超然境界。

武当山宫观道乐是我国秦巴地区优秀民间文化与唐代至明代宫廷音乐相结合的产物，具有庄严典雅的气质，醇厚浓郁的韵味，南北交集的特色，佛道融合的宗教色彩，极大地拓宽了民族音乐学科，是我国民族音乐的瑰宝，被列入国家非物质文化遗产名录。在历史的传承中，武当山宫观道乐不仅融合了其它宗派道乐的精华，还汲取了中国民间音乐的精髓；不但具有古代巴楚音乐的苍劲浑厚，又飘逸出宫廷音乐的优雅风韵，演奏中无不散发出浓郁的宗教色彩和古典韵味。武当山宫观道乐经过数百年的孕育、发展，既有中国道教音乐的共性，又有其独特的个性，集多源性、融摄性、延续性、保守性为一体。它那优美动听的旋律、神秘奇特的美感，具有很强的感染力和渗透力，不但能陶冶情操，还能给人以清心、静心的玄妙感受。

In Wudang Museum, listening to the Wudang Taoist music, your heart will pure.
Wudang Taoist music is the product of the combination of folk culture of Qin-ba area and the palace music of Tang Dynasty to the Ming Dynasty. As the national music treasure, it has been listed as the national non-material cultural heritage which has broadened the national music subject. It has elegant quality, unique feature of the mix of south and north culture and the religion cultural confluent of Buddhism and Taoism. In historical inheritance, Wudang Taoist music is not only mix together with the essence of other religion faction music but also absorb the quintessence of Chinese folk music. Going through hundreds of years' development, it has the general character of Taoist music but also has unique features. It has fair-sounding melody, fancy sensibility feeling and powerful infection which can cultivate your taste, pure your heart and give peace.

宫观道乐厅
Taoist Music Hall

引 言
Preface

　　武当山宫观道乐源远流长。东汉末年，道教五斗米教诞生不久，由蜀地汉中经由武当山四面传播。武当山地区的五斗米教神祀仪式"其设颇雄"。这种神祀活动通常以巫祝利用歌舞的形式进行。古时的巫是通过歌舞作为"娱神"、"降神"而达到祈福的目的。这种师巫而舞的形式对宫观道乐中的踏罡布斗，走"禹步"有着深远的影响。

　　南北朝时期，北魏帝王崇信道教，在华山、蒿山修行的著名道士寇谦之对道教进行了大幅的改革，要求天下道徒"一从吾乐章诵诫新法"。在寇谦之完善的道教科仪中设坛诵经是道教音乐又一发展时期。特别是将直诵道经改为乐诵，即念经改为唱经。武当山因北方饱学之士不断入山采乐，寇谦之这种仙音天成的乐章也随之广为传唱。

　　唐宋时期，武当山有影响的社会活动日益增多。贞观年间，均州太守姚简设坛祈雨成功，武当山因而受到特别关注，唐太宗遂敕建五龙祠。不久，唐宗室失意者不断贬居武当山地区的房县及郧县，唐宫廷音乐也被带到了武当山。

　　五代陈抟熟读经史，音乐修养极高，常"行歌坐乐，日游市肆"。陈抟曾在武当山修道二十余年，练"五龙睡法"，其"睡有乐"，很可能是一种催眠曲。南宋高宗赵构诏武当山主持孙寂然赴临安皇宫设醮唱道，不但将武当山的道乐引进宫廷，同时，也将宫廷雅乐带回武当山，这些对武当山道乐的发展产生了深远的影响。

　　元代诸帝推崇真武神，特别是元仁宗与真武生日相同，故每逢圣诞，必在武当山设醮祝贺。仁宗后，这种为皇帝生日建醮的形式有增无减，甚至一年多达四次。这种由皇室直接安排的唱经、诵经和道教歌舞不但规模大、档次高，而且影响深远。

　　明代是武当山道乐最辉煌的时期。明初，太祖朱元璋设立玄教院管理全国道教，洪武十五年（1382），改为道录司，隶属礼部。设神乐观，以道士冷谦定雅乐。明成祖朱棣登基，大修武当，功成作乐，亲自撰写《大明御制玄教乐章》，供武当山道士演唱，并敕令神乐观派400名乐舞生充实到武当山道观。这种史无前例的举动，将武当山宫观道乐提升为宫廷雅乐，成为当时最重要的音乐盛事。同时，也确定了武当山的宫观道乐在中国音乐史上的特殊地位。明代后期，武当山宫观道乐开始逐步趋向民间音乐形式。

　　清代，由于武当山道教由官方深入民间，朝山进香活动已成为河南、四川、湖北、陕西等省乡民的习俗，吹吹打打的朝山队伍，将各地民间音乐带到武当山，武当山道乐进一步世俗化。从武当山道乐流行的曲牌来看，清代和民国流行的曲调居多，有些道乐除使用道教经卷和保持乐器组合及演奏规则之外，乐曲的风格已和民间音乐没有多大的区别。

　　民国时，由于社会不稳定，道众或出走或还俗，通经乐者已不多，盛极一时的武当山道乐几乎声断音消。

　　解放后，特别是武当山对外开放以来，党和政府对武当道乐进行了抢救性的挖掘、整理、开发、利用。1986年春，在"全国民族音乐集成"工作的推动下，湖北省文化厅、武汉音乐学院抽调专家组织专班对武当山宫观道乐进行了全面、系统的搜集、整理，编辑出版了《中国武当山道教音乐》一书，这是第一部中国道教音乐的专著，对推动中国宗教音乐的发展起到重要作用。同时，依托武汉音乐学院等高等院校为武当山培养一大批道教音乐人才，使道乐水平有了较大提高。1987年，在武当山召开了全国民族民间器乐曲宗教寺庙音乐会，到会专家对武当山道乐给予充分肯定，认为它是我国的宝贵遗产。武当山特区工委、管委会为传承、弘扬武当山道乐，专门成立宗教事务局，负责包括武当山道乐在内的武当文化的挖掘、整理。

　　武当山道乐，在近千年的历史传延中，既融合了其它道派的道乐，又汲取了南北民间音乐的精华，既吸纳了古代巴楚音乐的苍劲浑厚，又富蕴宫廷音乐的优雅、风韵，或激扬，或婉转，或肃穆，或清新，在道人的演奏下散发出浓郁的宗教色彩和古典韵味。由武汉音乐学院教授史新民主编的《武当山道教音乐》一书认为，武当山宫观道乐，从整体构成上看，主要成分是古代音乐、宫廷音乐和艺术性较为成熟的民间音乐；其形态和风格的一般特征，主要偏重我国南方尤其是江南一带音乐的风格色彩；课诵（早晚坛）音乐是道乐的主要代表，从其曲名、形态、风格特征来看，它是最纯正的道教自己的音乐类型，保存了道教音乐中最古老的曲调。武当山宫观道乐经过千余年的孕育、形成、发展，既有中国道教音乐的共性，又有独特的个性，具有多源性、融摄性、延续性和保守性。

Wudang Taoist music has a long history. In the last years of the Eastern Han Dynasty, the Taoist five-dou-rice school comes into being and spread from the Hanzhong of Shan Xi province to the Wudang Mountain. In Wudang Mountain, the five-dou-rice school usually offer sacrifices to the gods in dance. In ancient times, the one who do the offering usually through songs and dance to pray which has a profound influence to the dance of Taoist music.

During the Northern and Southern Dynasties, the emperor of the Northern Wei Dynasty respect Taoism, a famous Taoist priest reform Taoism requiring all Taoist priests sing the Taoist classical books which is the develop period for Taoist music. Many learned scholars come to Wudang Mountain to learn the music.

In the Tang and Song Dynasties, there are many influential social activities in Wudang Mountain. In the Zhen Guan years of Tang Dynasty, Yao Jian, the prefecture chief of Jun Zhou, pray for rain and it worked which make Wudang Mountain got close attention and built Five-dragon Ancestral Temple. Later, many imperial clans have been degraded to Fang Xian County and Yun Xian County that the palace music of Tang Dynasty has been taken into Wudang Mountain.

Chen Tuan living in the Five Dynasty reads over historical books and is good at music. When he cultivated himself in Wudang Mountain for more than 20 years, he created the five dragon sleeping way with music which is probably a kind of cradlesong. In the Southern Song Dynasty, the Emperor Zhao Kou ask Sun Jiran, the Taoist host of Wudang Mountain to the imperial palace give rite which bring Taoist music to the palace. Meanwhile, it takes the imperial gagaku to Wudang Mountain which has a far-reaching influence to Wudang Mountain.

In the Yuan Dynasty, the emperors worship God Zhen Wu, especially the emperor Ren Zong who has the same birthday with Zhen Wu. Thus, every birthday, there are celebrate rites in Wudang Mountain. After that, there are many rites holding in Wudang Mountain for celebrating emperors' birthday. Sometimes, there are four rites within one year. This kind of rite which is arranged by imperial family has large scale, high grade and profound influence.

The Ming Dynasty is the glorious period for Wudang Taoist music. In the beginning of Ming Dynasty, the emperor Zhu Yuanzhang sent Xuan Jiao Yuan to take charge of the national Taoism. Then the Emperor Zhu Di built Wudang on a large scale and composed music by himself to Wudang Taoist priests and send 400 musicians to temples and palaces in Wudang Mountain. This is unprecedented that making Wudang Taoist music graded as palace gagaku which becoming the most important music at that time. Meanwhile, it made sure Wudang Taoist music has the special position in the history of Chinese music. In the later period of Ming Dynasty, the Wudang Taoist music tends to folk music.

In Qing Dynasty, owing to Wudang Taoism spread from the official to the folk, going on a pilgrimage is a custom such as He Nan, Si Chuan, Hu Bei and Shan Xi. The pilgrimage people bring folk music of different places to Wudang Mountain which makes Wudang Taoist music more secularization. From the popular Wudang Taoist music, the most tune are in Qing Dynasty and the republic of China. Some Taoist music has the same style with the folk music except the Taoist instruments and play rules.

In the republic of China, due to the instability of the society, the Taoist priests leave the temple or resume secular life, and the Wudang music nearly disappear.

After the liberation, especially the policy of Wudang Mountain opening to the outside, the CCP and government exploit and utilize Wudang music. In the spring of 1986, thanks to the edition of the National Music Integration, the experts from Culture Department of Hubei Province and Wuhan Conservatory of Music published the national first monograph *Chinese Wudang Mountain Taoist Music* which played important role to the development of Chinese relational music. Meanwhile, many colleges and universities such as Wuhan Conservatory of Music train many musicians who are good at Taoist music. In 1987, Wudang Mountain holds the religion concert of national folk music. The music experts who attend the concert give high praise to the Wudang Taoist music taking it as national treasure. To inherit and carry on Wudang Taoist music, the Wudang Mountain work committee and the management committee set up Bureau of Religious Affairs mainly in charge of developing Wudang culture including Taoist music.

Wudang Taoist music is the combination of folk music and palace music. Some melodies are elegance, some are solemn, some are inspirit and some are pure. It has religion color and classical flavor played by Taoist priests. In the book *Wudang Mountain Taoist Music*, edited by Professor Shi Xinmin from Wuhan Conservatory of Music, the Wudang Taoist music is mainly ancient music, palace music and folk music. The style is mainly inclined to the south of the nation especially the south region of the Yangtze River. The music used in the morning and evening class is the major representative of Taoist music which is the pure Taoist music style and conserved the oldest melody of Taoist music. Wudang Taoist music not only has the common characteristics of Chinese Taoist music but also the unique feature of its own.

【木鱼】

打击乐器。原为佛教"梵吹"的伴奏乐器，亦为法器之一。木鱼多半呈团鱼形，腹部中空，头部正中开口，尾部盘绕，其状昂首缩尾，背部呈斜坡形，两侧三角形，底部椭圆。武当山有二种，一种为长方形，木质槌，槌头为橄榄形；一种为鱼形。

在民族乐队中，备有音高不同、数量不等的成套木鱼，按五声、七声音阶或十二平均律排列组合，常用于轻快活泼的乐曲中，有时可独奏简短的乐句，或用来模仿马蹄声的音响效果。木鱼在我国很早就出现了，但是有记载的历史却比较晚。这种特殊的器物，并非只在寺庙中才能够见到。早在明清时期，木鱼就已经用于宫廷音乐、昆曲以及民间音乐的演奏。

The wooden fish

It is a kind of percussive instrument. It was originally the musical instrument for the accompaniment of the Buddhist "Fanchui" (a kind of religious music), and it was also one of the Buddhist instruments. Most of the wooden fishes are ball-shaped and hollowed, with the center of the head mouth-opened and the end tangled. It holds up its head and hides its end. Its back (the percussive part) is a slope, its two sides are of a triangle shape, and its base is an ellipse. As to the wooden fish in the Wudang Mountains, there are two kinds. One is rectangular, with a wooden short club having an olive-shaped club head. The other is shaping like fish.

In the national band, there are many sets of wooden fishes with different pitches and different quantity, grouped in accordance with the five-voice-part and seven-voice-part musical scale or the twelve average rhythms. They are usually used in the lively music, sometimes performing the solo of some short musical sentence, and sometimes imitating the horses' clop. The wooden fish has appeared very early, but its recording history is relatively late. This special instrument not only can be seen in the temple. Actually early to the time of the Ming Dynasty and the Qing Dynasty, it has been used in the performance of the court music, the Kunqu opera, and the folk music.

【鲸鱼】

鲸鱼具有双重功用，既可当钟杵，亦可做木鱼，其在道教中并不多见，至今全国发现仅此一件。《文选》记载："于是发鲸鱼，铿华钟。"唐李善注，引薛综曰："海中有大鱼曰鲸，海边又有兽名蒲牢。……蒲牢素畏鲸，鲸鱼击蒲牢，辄大鸣。凡钟欲令声大者，故作蒲牢于上，所以撞之者为鲸鱼。"后因以"蒲牢"为钟的别名。该鲸鱼原藏武当山南岩天乙真庆宫内，制于明代，木质，全长106cm，厚16.1cm，腹高16cm，重20.3kg。鲸鱼嘴巴张开呈袭击嘶咬蒲牢状，嘴唇短平，眼、鳃、鳍、尾完备，整件鲸鱼雕制工艺简练，刻画了"发鲸鱼，铿华钟"的生动形象。

Whale

It has two functions, as the striker and as the wooden fish. It is rarely seen in Taoism. There is only one whale in the whole country until now. Then why the Taoism uses the whale? According to *Ban Gu in the Anthology*, it says that "then a whale was sent to strike the Hua bell", noted by Li Shan in the Tang Dynasty. Xue Zong (from the State of Wu during the Three Kingdoms era) said, "There was a big fish named whale in the sea, and there was also an animal named Pulao along the coast. Pulao was always afraid of the whale. When the whale attacked Pulao, Pulao shouted loudly. Since any bell wants its sound be loud, people carve the pattern of Pulao onto it, and call the striker the whale". Later Pulao becomes the bell's byname. This whale was originally preserved in the Tianyizhenqing Palace of South Crag in Wudang Mountains, 106cm long, 16.1cm thick, and 20.3kg. It opens its mouth posturing like to attack and bite Pulao, with short and flat lips and complete eyes, gills, fins, and tails. It is of simple carving technique, forming the vivid image of "sending the whale to strike the Hua bell".

【如意铁磬】

道教礼乐器。明永乐十三年御赐大岳太和山五龙宫。该铁磬通高96cm，宽86cm，重60.1kg。其整体呈如意形，正面中部阳铸"敕建大岳太和山兴圣五龙宫"字样，背面正中阳铸"大明永乐十三年九月吉日造"字样。

道家建醮道场，演行法事时，必振金钟玉磬，敲击玉磬，铿锵琳琅之音，可上彻云霄，下震尘寰。古代，磬为击奏乐器，质地多为玉质，最早用于先民的乐舞活动，后来为历代帝王的殿堂宴享、宗庙祭祀、朝聘礼仪活动中的乐队演奏所用，成为象征其身份地位的重要礼乐器。

The ruyi iron chime stone

It is a Taoist rites musical instrument, bestowed by the emperor to the Five-dragon Palace in the great high Taihe Mountain in the 13th year of Yongle's reign in the Ming Dynasty. It is made in Ming Dynasty. It is iron made shaping like Ruyi with the height of 96cm, 86cm wide and 60.1kg. In the middle of the front carved the Chinese characters means this is for the Five Dragon Palace. And in the middle of the back the Chinese characters tell that this is made in September of the 13th year of Yongle regin.

When Taoism builds Taoist rites and holds religious ceremony, the gold bell and the jade chime stone will be definitely stricken. The clanging sound of striking the jade chime stone could penetrate the cloud and the earth. In ancient times, the chime stone is a kind of percussive instrument in jade quality. It was originally used in the musical activities of ancestors, and later it is used in the band performance when in the royal feast, the religious sacrificing and the court engaging activities which symbolizing the status.

【永乐铁铸双龙钮钟】

道教礼乐器。铁质，明永乐二十二年四月（1424）铸，通高94cm，口径69cm，重70kg。钟身阳铸楷书："甲辰岁永乐二十二年孟夏月大吉日造"字样。钟钮双龙拱背相接，两首逆向，四爪，螭首俱接钟体。拱背下为悬钟钮洞孔。溜肩，有凸纹两圈，钟体对称凸纹方框四。方框下为凸纹四道，每两方框间下，有一凸纹圆形击打点，将四道凸纹隔断。钟口外侈，为波浪形，八足，有凸纹装饰纹四，凸形、波纹圈一道。

该钟整体造型端庄，古朴典雅。钟钮形象为蒲牢，传说中为龙王第四子，性好鸣，故将其放置到钟上。道教在做法事时希望钟声悠扬，传说蒲牢畏鲸，所以人们就将钟杵做成鲸的式样，受击后蒲牢就大声吼叫，充作洪钟提梁的兽钮，助其鸣声远扬。

The Yongle iron bell

It is a Taoist rites musical instrument, iron, built in April in the 22nd year of Yongle's reign in the Ming Dynasty. It is 94cm high, 69cm with its caliber and 70kg weight. There are carved Chinese characters which record the date of making. The two dragons on the upper part of the bell lean back each other; four hands hold the body of the bell. There is a hole under the top part which is for hanging the bell. There are decorations on the body of the bell. And the mouth is shaped like wave with eight angles and decorations.

It simple and elegant, the upper part of the bell is of the Pulao's image, which is the fourth son of the dragon king. It favors shouting, so it is placed on the bell. Taoism hopes the sound of the bell could be melodious. In the legend, Pulao was afraid of the whale, so people made the bell striker into a whale's shape as the upper part of the bell which is related with the girder by a rope in order to help make the sound louder and spread further.

【磬】

道教礼乐法器，中国古代乐器之一，起源很早，发展到秦更趋完善。在中国特殊的文化传统中，它不但是乐器，同时也与政治礼制联系在一起，形成一套礼乐文化。在道教祭祀活动中，击磬即为通知神灵，使人、神心灵感应。该磬铁质，清康熙四十一年铸造，口径49cm，通高44.2cm，重58.9kg。

The chime stone

The chime stone is one of the ancient musical instruments in China. It has a very early origin, and develops into maturity until the Qin Dynasty. In the special cultural tradition of China, it is not only a musical instrument, but also representing a set of the musical culture for having some relations with the political rites system. In Taoist worshiping activities, the striking of the chime stone means the communicating with the deity. It was made in Qing Dynasty, iron. Its caliber is 49cm with the height of 44.2cm and 58.9kg.

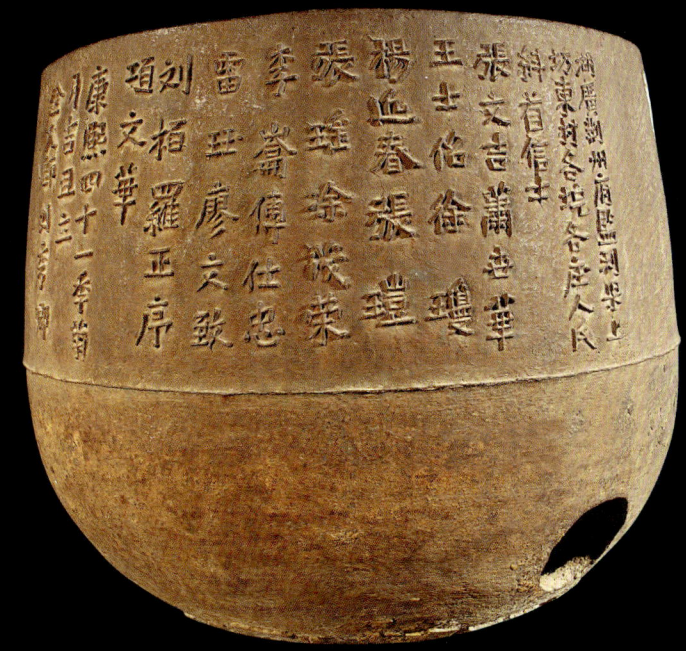

【法衣】

法衣是方丈、高功、经师在作法事时所穿的衣服。常作对襟，有宽镶边，多为紫红色，绣有龙、云鹤、八卦、八宝等纹饰。该法衣为民国年间制，绸，长136cm，宽155cm，重0.9kg。

The cassock

The cassock is the clothes worn by the Taoist priests when they are conducting Taoist ceremony. It is usually a jacket with buttons straight down the front, embroidered with broad band, mostly purplish red, decorated some patterns of dragon, cloud crane, the Eight Diagrams, the eight treasure objects, etc.. It was made in the Republic of China (1912-1949), silk, 136cm long, 155cm wide and 0.9kg weight.

【铛】

铛又称"单音"、"铜铛"等,俗称"铛子",是把小铜锣固定在长柄的木框上,用拨子敲打出声。如果是十面小锣固定于同一木架,安上长柄,则称"云锣"或"云鏊"。该铛为民国年间制,铜质,口径14.7cm,高3.8cm,重0.3kg。

Dang

Dang is also called "danyin" or "tongdang", conventionally named "dangzi". It is a small gong fixed on a wooden frame with a long handle, stricken by the striker to produce sound. If there are ten small gongs fixed on a same wooden shelf, with a long handle installed, then it will be called "yunluo" or "yun'ao". It is made in the Republic of China (1912-1949), copper, with caliber of 14.7cm and 3.8cm high, 0.3kg weight.

【钹】

钹亦名"铜盘",一般为铜质,形状是中央隆起的圆片,在其隆起部位系有红布条。有大小之别:大的称为"饶钹"、"闹钹"或"大钹",小的称为"钗"或"钗子"。击打时双手各持一片的布条,合击发声,也有的把一片置于圆形的凹状布垫上面,用另一片去击打。在道场上,通常和铛子配合使用。该钹为清朝年间制,铜质,口径66.6cm,一重6.5kg,一重5.5kg。

The cymbals

The cymbals are also called "the copper plate", usually made of copper. In the center, there is a hunch for each, and on each hunch, there ties a red strip of cloth. The bigger cymbals are called "naobo" or "big cymbals", and the smaller ones are called "cha" or "chazi". When striking, people hold the strip of cloth in each hand, and make sound by striking them to each other. On Taoist rites, the cymbals are usually used together with dangzi. They are made in Qing Dynasty, copper, with the caliber of 66.6cm. One is weight 6.5kg, the other is 5.5kg.

【铃】

铃又名"三清铃"、"摇铃"、"帝钟"、"法钟"、"法铃"等。一般为铜制,有柄,铃内有舌,摇动发声。柄的上端为"山"字形,象征道教信奉的三清尊神。道教认为,法铃具有降妖、除魔的作用。在道场上使用时,须以单手持之,向一边有节奏地摇动。该铃为民国年间制,铜质,其中一铃口径6cm,高3.6cm,重0.1kg;另一铃口径5cm,高3.2cm,重0.1kg。

The small bell

The small bell is also called "the sanqing small bell", "the waving small bell", "the di bell", "the fa bell", "the fa small bell", and so on. It is usually made of copper, handled, with a tongue-like object in the small bell, producing sound when people waving it. The upper part of the handle is shaped like the Chinese word "Shan", symbolizing the sanqing deity worshiped by Taoism. Taoism believes that the religious small bell has the effect of destroying the evil. When it is used in the Taoist rites, it should be held by only one hand, and be waved rhythmically towards one direction. The bell is made in the Republic of China (1912-1949), copper, one is 6cm of the caliber, 3.6 cm high, 0.1kg weight. The other is 5cm of the caliber, 3.2cm high, 0.1kg weight.

【二胡】

二胡又名胡琴，始于唐朝，乐器的一种，至今已有一千多年的历史。它最早发源于我国古代北方地区的一个少数民族，那时叫"奚琴"。在道教音乐演奏中，二胡与笙、笛都是主要的乐器。

Erhu

Erhu (the Chinese two-stringed musical instrument) is also called huqin, appeared in the Tang Dynasty, one kind of musical instrument, with a more-than-one-thousand-year history. It was first originated from an ancient minority in the northern part of our country, and it was named "xiqin" at that time. In the Taoist musical performance, erhu, sheng and the flute are the main musical instruments.

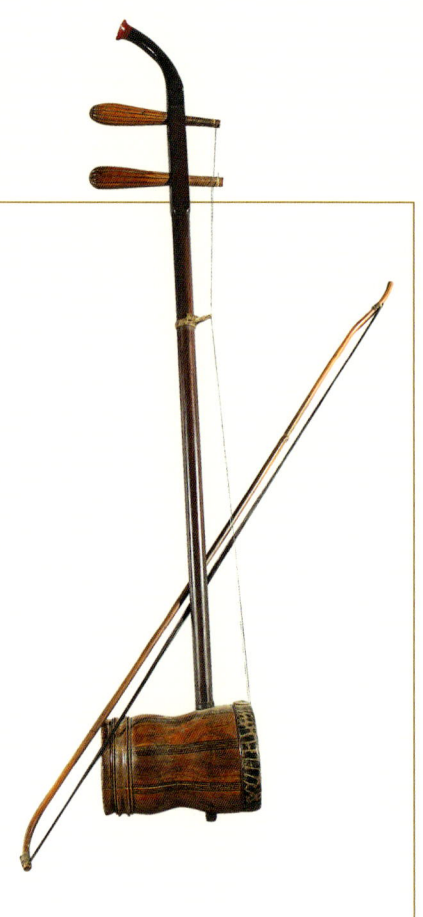

【笛子】

笛子是中国广为流传的吹奏乐器，因为是用天然竹材制成，所以也称为"竹笛"。笛子虽然短小简单，但它却有七千年的历史。在民族乐演奏中笛子也是不可缺少的乐器。笛子的表现力非常丰富，它既能演奏悠长、高亢的旋律，又能表现辽阔、宽广的情调，同时也可以奏出欢快华丽的舞曲和婉转优美的小调。

The flute

The flute is a very popular wind musical instrument of China. Since it is made of bamboo, it is also called "the bamboo flute". Although short and simple, it has a seven-thousand-year history. In the national musical performance, it is also indispensable. It has a rich expressive power. It can perform the long and loud music, it can express the sentiment of expansion and width, and it also can perform the bright and magnificent dance music, as well as the sweet and elegant ditty.

【箫】

箫也称为洞箫，是中国古老的气鸣乐器。早在几千年前，箫就在中国民间流传了。关于它的来历，要从排箫说起。排箫在几千年前刚形成的时候，它就被称为箫。后来人们在吹排箫的过程中，发现在一支管子上开出距离不等的孔，也能吹出高低不同的声音，于是箫逐渐由多管组成的排箫，演变为单管数孔的洞箫。

今天的箫在汉代就有了，但当时被称为"羌笛"。羌笛原为居住在四川、甘肃一带的羌族人民的乐器，公元前1世纪时流传到黄河流域，经过发展，逐渐演变成六孔，和今天的箫非常相似。

箫的构造比较简单，形状和笛子非常相像。它一般用紫竹、黄枯竹或者白竹制作。管身比笛子稍长一点，顶端用竹簧封口，封口的边缘上开有一个吹孔。管身正面有五个音孔，背面靠上的部位还有一个音孔。另外，管身下端的背部还有三到四个出音孔和助音孔，用来调整音准，美化音色和增大音量。

箫的音色柔和、典雅，低音区发音深沉，弱奏时很有特色；中音区音色圆润、优美。箫的演奏技巧基本上和笛子相同，但它的灵活程度远不如笛子，不宜表现快捷花哨的内容，只适合于吹奏悠长细腻、恬静抒情的曲调，多用来表现大自然的美景和抒发人物的内心情感。箫的表现力很丰富，它可以用于独奏、重奏和合奏，还用于江南丝竹、福建南音、广东音乐等民间器乐乐种里，另外它还用于一些地方戏曲的伴奏。

Xiao

Xiao (the Chinese bamboo flute) is also called dongxiao, an ancient blowing instrument of China. Early to several thousand years ago, it has already been popular in the folk China. It begins from paixiao. When paixiao was just formed several thousand years ago, it was called xiao. Later when people were playing paixiao, they found that if they made some holes with different distances from each other on a pipe, they can also produce the sound with different pitches. So xiao evolved from paixiao which is composed of many pipes into dongxiao which is a pipe with several holes.

Today's xiao has appeared in the Han Dynasty, at that time named "qiangdi". Qiangdi was originally the musical instrument of the Qiang people in Sichuan and Gansu provinces. In the 1st century B.C., it came down to the Yellow River Basin, and gradually developed into one with six holes which is similar to today's xiao.

Xiao has a simple structure, similar to the flute. It is commonly made of the black bamboo, the huangku bamboo, or the white bamboo. It is a little bit longer than the flute, sealed by the bamboo joint on top with a blowing hole on the verge. There are five sound holes in the front part of the pipe, and another hole in the upper part of the pipe's back. In addition, in lower part of the pipe's back, there are three to four sound holes and assistant sound holes which are used to adjust the tone, beautify the tone, and increase the volume.

Xiao has a gentle and elegant tone color, with the bourdon low and distinctive, and the mediant smooth and beautiful. The performing technique of xiao is similar to that of the flute, but its flexibility is not as good as the flute. It is not suitable to perform the lively music, but the long, exquisite, quiet, and lyrical melody. It is mostly used to express the beauty of the nature and the innermost emotion of the character. It has a rich expressive power. It can be used in solo, ensemble, and tutti, and in sizhu (an ensemble of stringed and woodwind instrument) of the south of the lower Yangtze River, Nanyin of Fujian Province, and the Cantonese music, and other folk music as well. It also can be used as the accompaniment of some local traditional opera.

【笙】

笙是中国非常古老的簧管乐器。殷商时期的甲骨文中已有"和"（小笙）的名称。春秋战国时期，笙已非常流行，它与竽并存，在当时不仅是为声乐伴奏的主要乐器，而且也有合奏、独奏的形式。南北朝到隋唐时期，竽、笙仍并存应用，但竽一般只用于雅乐，而笙却被广泛应用。早期的笙为竹制，后来改为铜制。明清时期，民间流传的笙有方、圆、大、小各种不同的形制。笙的音色明亮甜美，高音清脆透明，中音柔和丰满，低音浑厚低沉，音量较大，而且在中国传统吹管乐器中，也是唯一能够吹出和声的乐器。在和其它乐器合奏的时候，能起到调和乐队音色、丰富乐队音响的作用。

Sheng

Sheng is a very ancient reed pipe instrument of China. In the inscriptions on bones or tortoise shells of the Yin Dynasty, there has already been the name of "he" (the name for the small sheng). In the Spring and Autumn period and the Warring States, sheng has become very popular, and existed with yu. At that time, it was not only the main musical instrument for accompaniment, but it also has the form of tutti and solo. From the Northern and Southern Dynasty to the Sui and Tang Dynasty, yu and sheng are still used together. However, yu is commonly used for the ceremonial classic music, and sheng was used widely. The early sheng was made of bamboo, and later it is copper-made. In the Ming and Qing Dynasty, the civil sheng has different forms, square, round, large, and small. The tone color of sheng is bright and sweet, with the alt ringing and pure, the mediant gentle and rich, and the bourdon thick, low, and loud. Moreover, among the Chinese traditional blowpipe musical instruments, it is the only one that can produce harmony. When played with other musical instruments, it can adjust the tone into consonance and enrich the sound of the band.

宫观道乐厅 204-205
Taoist Music Hall

铜锣 gong 平鼓 flat drum 手鼓 tambourine 唢呐 suona horn

鼓 drum

宫观道乐厅
Taoist Music Hall

宫观道乐厅
Taoist Music Hall

后 记

　　武当博物馆在国家、省、市等各级领导的高度重视与关心下，已于2008年4月23日正式向海内外游客免费开放。博物馆自开放以来，受到了各级领导以及社会各界的普遍好评，原国家文物局局长张文彬先生则用"三个没想到"给予了武当博物馆高度的评价，即"没想到武当山道教文物这么丰富！没想到武当山道教造像这么多！没想到武当山道教文物等级这么高！"

　　为了更好地弘扬武当文化，进一步加大对武当博物馆馆藏文物的研究及其文化内涵的挖掘，我馆从2009年开始，以《神韵——武当道教造像艺术》一书为起点，拟分别从道教造像、书法、绘画、彩绘、壁画、砖雕、木雕、石雕、真武传说、文物背后的故事等不同角度，按照雅俗共赏的原则，出版一套《武当博物馆系列丛书》。

　　《太和武当》（武当博物馆道教文化展）一书原计划在开馆前期就编撰出版，但由于各种原因未能实现。为了使观众能够更加全面深入地了解武当道教文化展的精髓，经多方努力，我馆抽调精干力量，终于顺利完成了该书的编纂工作。

　　在本书的编辑过程中，为了能够适合不同层次读者的口味，能给每位读者以最直观的感受，书稿尽量图文并茂，以便向读者展示武当道教文化展的精髓。对于书中的某些观点和提法，读者如有不同意见，望不吝赐教。

　　本书的出版，得到了文物出版社、武当山旅游经济特区管委会的大力支持，武当山旅游经济特区工委书记李发平同志主编并作序。在文物拍摄过程中，得到了武当博物馆全体职工的积极配合。在此，我们对长期以来关心、支持武当山文物保护事业的各级领导、同志一并表示最诚挚的谢意！同时，我们也衷心地祝愿武当山明天更美好！

编 者

2011年7月

Postscript

Attached great importance and concern at all levels of national, provincial and municipal leaders, Wudang Museum officially opened free of charge to visitors at home and abroad on 23, April 2008. Since the opening up of our Museum, leaders at all levels and personage of various circles have a rather high opinion of the Museum. Former director of State Cultural Relics Bureau Zhang Wenbin gave Wudang Museum high prize: "I never expect that Wudang Mountain has so rich Taoist cultural relics, so many Taoist josses, so high-rank of the cultural level."

In order to promote the Wudang Culture preferable and further research on the collection of cultural relics and excavate its cultural connotation, our Museum plan to publish a set of books named Wudang Museum Series suit both refined and popular tastes, which will include Taoist joss, calligraphy, painting, color drawing, murals, brick sculptural, wood carving, stone carving, legends of Zhen Wu and the stories of the cultural relics. Last year, we've already published the picture album of *Shen Yun Wudang Taoist Josses Art*.

Due to various reasons, the book *Taihe Wudang Cultural Exhibition of Wudang Museum* which supposed to be published before the museum to be used, has been come off the press. With the efforts of all staffs in the Museum, this book is finished to let the visitors learn the pith of Taoist culture comprehensively and profoundly.

During the edition of this book, to suit the taste of readers at different levels, this book includes both pictures and captions which will give every reader the most direct display. However, due to limited space, the Taoist culture can not be displayed comprehensively. Reference to some of the arguments, for the reader who has different views, we be expected to accept the analysis and correction.

The publication of this book has got strong support by all levels of management, especially the Chinese Heritage Press and Wudang Mountain Tourism and Economic Special Zone. Secretary of Wudang Mountain Tourism and Economic Special Zone Li Faping has written the preface for this book. In the process of photograph, the whole museum work hard and overtime for the completion of the shooting. We'd like to express our sincere thanks to the leaders and departments at all levels that are long-standing interest in and support Wudang cultural relic conservation. Meantime, we also sincerely wish Wudang Mountain will have a better tomorrow.

Editor

July, 2011